THE INVISIBLE VICTIM

THE

INVISIBLE

VICTIM

THE CRIMINAL JUSTICE SYSTEM'S FORGOTTEN RESPONSIBILITY

ROBERT REIFF

Basic Books, Inc., Publishers   New York

Permission to reprint material from the following sources is gratefully acknowledged:

Norval Morris and Gordon Hawkins, *The Honest Politician's Guide to Crime Control* (Chicago: University of Chicago Press, 1970), pp. 87, 90, and 91.

Del Martin, *Battered Wives* (San Francisco: Glide Publications, 1976), pp., 90, 91, 92, and 105. Copyright © 1976 by Del Martin. Published by Glide Publications.

Stephen Schafer, *Compensation and Restitution to Victims of Crime* (Montclair, N. J.: Paterson, Smith, 1970), p. 8, 121, 128–129.

New York State Crime Victims Compensation (CVCB), *1976–1977 A Review of the Tenth Year of Operation,* pp. 4 and 8.

Excerpts from the following articles are reprinted by permission of The New York Times Company. Copyright © 1976 and 1977 by the New York Times Company: Emanuel Perlmutter, "Couple, Recently Robbed, Take Their Lives Citing Fear," *New York Times,* 17 Oct. 1976, p. 51; Robert D. MacFadden, *New York Times,* 14 July 1977, p. A1; Robert D. McFadden, *New York Times,* 15 July 1977, p. A1; *New York Times,* 27 May 1977, p. A9; "Justice Dept. May Create New Crime-Report Agency," *New York Times,* 20 Apr. 1977, p. 19; Judy Klemesrud, *New York Times,* 12 Nov. 1976, p. B6; Gerald Astor, "Crime Doesn't Pay Its Victims Very Well Either," *New York Times,* 30 May 1976, p. E9; Judy Klemesrud, *New York Times,* 13 Nov. 1976, p. 11; Leslie Maitland, "10 Rape Victims Identify Youth They All Feared to See Again," *New York Times,* 24 May 1977, p. 1; Lesley Oelsner, "Coleman Asserts Bar Fails Public," *New York Times,* 8 Aug. 1976, p. 25; Fred Ferretti, "Crimes Against Elderly Bring Aged and Youths Into Court as Monitors," *New York Times,* 28 July 1977, p. B2; Donald G. McNeil, Jr., "Carter Approves Emergency Help for Love Canal," *New York Times,* 8 Aug. 1978, p. A1.

Library of Congress Cataloging in Publication Data

Reiff, Robert, 1913–
. The invisible victim.

Includes bibliographical references and index.
1. Victims of crimes—United States. 2. Reparation—United States. I. Title.
HV6250.3.U5R44   362.8′8′0973   78–73970
ISBN: 0–465–03596–5

To My Family

June, Mark, Alfred, Gail, David, Eddie, and Eva

... without the victims' hatred of their oppressors the quest for justice lacks substance.

Harold Rosenberg[1]

CONTENTS

FOREWORD

The problem of crime always gets reduced to, "What can be done about criminals?" Nobody asks, "What can be done about victims?" Everyone assumes the best way to help the victim is to catch the criminal—as though the offender is the only source of the victim's troubles.

But the offender's criminal act is only the first scene in the victim's tragedy. *Once you become a victim of a violent crime you are launched on a career of social injustices, of callous post-crime victimization by the police, the courts, the legal profession, and the human service systems of the nation.*

Society—sensitive to the issues of social justice for the offender—spends millions of dollars on programs for offender-oriented court reform and rehabilitation. On the other hand, society fails to protect crime victims, degrades them socially, and refuses them aid.

The police are required by law to respect concrete and specific rights of offenders but they are blind to the rights of victims. These rights are generally left up to the discretionary decisions of the police—from which the victim has no appeal. If the police officer or district attorney decides not to make an arrest, or not to prosecute an offender, or to allow the offender to plea bargain his way out of the charge, the victim has no legal recourse.

The courts, too, conspire against victims by cheating them out of even the most civilized and socially accepted forms of retribution thus robbing them of a sense of justice.

The victim, innocent of any wrongdoing, deserves to be protected against loss. There can be no justice for victims until society acknowledges that a crucial principle of justice is *making the victim whole again.*

Instead, victims are considered a burden to society who have only themselves to blame for their plight. They are often left totally without resources—as completely devastated as victims of a natural disaster.

The human services system further degrades victims of violent crime—treating them like welfare clients and insisting they be reduced to pauperism before they are entitled to aid. Senseless and bewildering rules constantly penalize victims. Most social agencies are not responsive to the emergency nature of the victim's situation not because there are no funds but because of institutional policies and practices which define "emergencies" as the natural disasters of fire, floods, or earthquakes only.

Token restitution programs are launched and immediately founder on the corrections system's failure to provide work at realistic pay rates that would make restitution payments possible. Token state compensation laws are enacted that are bureaucratically rationed by failing to provide public information about them, restricting eligibility to paupers, and instituting application and investigative processes that may take as much as seven months before an award can be made.

Our cries against violence won't be taken seriously if we are indifferent to those who suffer it. From a practical viewpoint it is dangerous to be indifferent. Neglecting victims of violence communicates to the offender a lack of concern about violence itself. The offender interprets our indifference to victims as indifference to violence and becomes bolder. It doesn't do any good to talk about apprehending the offender as the best way to help the victim. For it takes the responsibility to aid victims out of the hands of society and places it in the hands of the police. Such a policy is political phrasemongering for the police haven't the responsibility, know-how, or resources to give victims the financial, medical, and legal aid they need.

Today's criminals feel their adversaries are the police and the courts, who, they quickly learn, often have a callous and dehumanized attitude toward victims. Not until criminals are convinced that victimizing someone will bring the wrath of all people—not just the police—will there be any successful impact on violent crime in the United States. Crime control will be more effective when criminals feel their adversaries are the ordinary citizens of the community, as well as the police and courts.

The agony of victims of violent crime is, indeed, a horror story: what happens to victims is not just an unfortunate accident, it is the result of social policies, practices, and procedures of the criminal justice system and human service agencies.

That is why I decided to write this book—to describe the mass tragedy of victims of violent crime and to suggest what we, as a nation and as individual citizens, can do about it; and to make the victim visible to the American public in the hope that once our citizens know what it is really like to be a victim of a violent crime, they will express their moral indignation in ways that will compel the city, state, and federal governments, as well as the public agencies, to respond to the desperate needs of victims.

When the social fog that makes victims invisible is lifted; when the full impact of injustice to victims of violent crime is known; when people realize there are more victims of criminals than of fires, floods, and earthquakes—they may want to do something to aid victims. Looking forward to that time I will propose a number of prescriptions designed to bring justice and aid to the invisible victim.

ACKNOWLEDGMENTS

I first became aware of the idea of a service for victims of crime through Georgette Bennett, now of NBC News, who at the time was a graduate student in sociology. My experience with the Crime Victims Service Center in the Bronx, New York, made this book possible. I am indebted therefore to the Mayor's Criminal Justice Coordinating Council that granted the funds from the Law Enforcement Assistance Administration. David Friedman, Associate Director of the Crime Victims Service Center, designed the computerized reporting system that provided important data about the needs of victims. He also contributed to the analysis and conceptualizations in the final report of that program. The dedication of the crime victims counselors—Yolanda Bako, Harmon X. Black, Lavora Elliott, Michael Handy, Ralph Martinez, Linda Monahan, and Raquel Rivera—contributed to our understanding of victims' problems. The cooperation and support of Captain Anthony Bouza, Bronx Borough Commander of the Police, was a significant factor in getting the Crime Victims Service Center started.

When the book began to take shape in my mind Bert Kruger Smith of the Hogg Foundation in Austin, Texas, read some draft chapters and encouraged me to continue. Mike Campbell, Debbie Edwards, Steve Englander, Terry Gilius, Dean Johnston, Maria and Hamlet Paoletti, Brian Rasmussen, and Diane and Jim Spearly—graduate students at the University of Texas—reacted to the ideas in the book with helpful suggestions. Dr. Josh Holahan, a colleague and friend, was an empathic sounding board during the writing. I am indebted to Glenn Martin who shared with me his research of State Crime Victims Compensation legislation in preparation for his master's thesis at the Lyndon Baines Johnson School of Public Affairs, University of Texas. The critique of chapter 5 by Attorney Lynn Sanders of

Acknowledgments

Austin, Texas, and the staff of AVID (Aid to Victims in Distress), a victim's assistance program in Austin, helped to clarify for me some of the legal and social aspects of the Bill of Rights for Victims. I am especially grateful to Jane Manaster, a writer and friend, who continually suggested material and graciously gave her time to critique the entire manuscript. Jennifer Brodkey Kaufman contributed to this book by her prompt and careful typing. June Gallessich, my wife, was a constant source of encouragement and support and contributed to the refinement of the concepts and ideas.

THE INVISIBLE VICTIM

CHAPTER 1

THE INVISIBLE DISASTER

It frightens me nobody seems to care about the innocent. When you read about a murder case, nobody seems to be horrified by the picture, say of a fragile old woman in a small cigarette shop, turning away to get a packet of cigarettes for a young thug, and being attacked and battered to death. No one seems to care about her terror and her pain, and the final merciful unconsciousness. Nobody seems to go through the agony of the *victim*. . . .

Agatha Christie[1]

Few experiences in life can equal the terror of being a victim of a violent crime. To be threatened with physical harm is frightening enough; when it actually happens it seems to be the ultimate catastrophe.

At one time or another you may have had an experience in which great physical harm might have come to you—a narrow escape from an accident that but for some fortunate circumstance might have been worse. Afterward, when you have time to think what might have happened, you break out in a cold sweat, your knees shake, you feel weak, nauseous. After a few moments you begin to calm down. The accident is over and you are safe, out of danger. The same feelings are experienced by victims of violent crime—with one significant difference. They cannot look back on the incident and calm themselves with the knowledge that the danger is over. They know that it can and probably will happen again. The state of shock, therefore, does not subside. Instead, fear increases and produces panic. It may take months to recover from the shock of a violent crime. Some may never fully recover from a chronic state of anxiety and near panic.

In the high-crime areas of the cities, it is not neurotic anxiety to live in terror once you become a victim of a violent crime. Hans and Emma Kable preferred death to living with fear.

NEWS ITEM[2]

Couple, Recently Robbed, Take Their Own Lives, Citing Fear

An elderly couple who were assaulted and robbed in their Bronx apartment last month hanged themselves from their bedroom doorknob after leaving a note saying that "we don't want to live in fear anymore."

The couple—Hans Kable, 78 years old, and his wife, Emma, 76—had laid out their best clothes on the bed of their neatly furnished apartment at 275 East 168th Street. . . .

Detectives of the Police Senior Citizens Robbery Unit said the couple had been robbed early last month, when Mr. Kable returned from shopping. . . .

In the handwritten note, which detectives translated from German, the elderly couple said that they had been the victims of crimes, that they had lived in the Morrisania neighborhood for many years and that they didn't want to leave.

The psychological trauma is worsened by the essential loneliness of the experience. No one can help you. You feel your destiny is entirely out of your hands. Whether you survive depends on the offender. You feel totally helpless, that you are absolutely unable to make the slightest effort to help yourself.

Violent crime occurs more often among the poor and socially disenfranchised, those for whom life itself is a constant struggle for survival. Imagine the catastrophe for people in these circumstances to be victimized. They suffer extensive and permanent injuries resulting in loss of earning potential and increased impoverishment for life. To the elderly these conditions are especially poignant for their bodies take longer to heal; they may never recover properly. In the case of murder or assault causing serious physical injury, entire families become victims of a single violent crime. Because you are poor, even relatively minor injuries, which for the middle class may be no more than inconveniences, are disasters. The cost of medical care can be catastrophic to those who are already medical indigents.

The loss of food and rent money may mean starvation, eviction, or the cutting off of utilities. The situation is often worsened by the offender, who threatens more serious harm if the crime is reported or prosecuted. Even if the offender is jailed, victims cannot be certain they are safe. In many cases threats are made by the offender's friends, relatives, or fellow gang members. The Reverend Daniel Nickerson, pastor of the Tried Stone Baptist Church in the Bronx, says: "The criminals, many as young as 12 and 13, prey on the elderly, because the elderly are often frail, vulnerable, unable to defend themselves and afraid to go to court because they fear retaliation."[3] "One thing that has puzzled the police and the public is the senseless violence that often accompanies the robbing of old people. Victims have been beaten, raped, set on fire, locked in closets and tortured to death."[4]

Most violent crime victims are concealed in the "undesirable" sections of the cities. The high-crime areas are the neighborhoods of the poor, those deteriorated urban streets that the majority of citizens avoid. What they know of poverty and crime comes from the media or from glimpses of these areas as they travel through them.

Victims also *make themselves* invisible. The realistic fear of revictimization accompanied by strong emotional shock often generates high levels of suspicion and distrust. Victims often isolate themselves, virtually hiding in their apartments, refusing to go out after daylight hours and avoiding interaction with strangers.

Mrs. Engelmann's life is pretty much like that of the other elderly people in her neighborhood. She spends most of the day at a senior citizens' center, walks home with a group of elderly people before it gets dark and then locks herself into her apartment for the evening. "Everybody's scared, everybody's afraid," she said. "But you ask yourself, 'What can you do?' When I go home and open the door at night, and I haven't been hurt, I say to myself, 'Thank God!' "[5]

These reactions become a permanent style of life.

Television and other media contribute to the victims' invisibility. Their customary way of dealing with crime is to focus exclusively on the offender, continually reinforcing the idea that what matters in crime is the game of cops and robbers. The victim is barely visible in the plot. The cast of characters consists of the "good guy" policeman and the "bad guy" offender. The major action takes place between them, the victim playing a bit part. Victims of violent crime, in life as well as in fiction, always play subordinate roles. Every day the public is led to believe that apprehending the offender is all there is to justice. After two or three hours of evening television, of watching "Kojak" or "Columbo," you can go to bed feeling safe because in the end justice always triumphs. Kojak is relentlessly savage to offenders but is kind, sympathetic, and considerate to victims. Kojak, like most of the other "good guys," gives us the feeling that the best and only way to help the victim and serve justice is to apprehend the offender. By the time the story ends, you have forgotten the victim because the apprehension of the offender has convinced you that the victim's needs have been met. But the real tragedy of victimization begins just where crime stories end. And at this point the victim becomes totally invisible.

Within the next thirty-one seconds someone, somewhere in the United States, will become a victim of a violent crime. If you live in a large metropolitan area, the chances are approximately one in seventy-five that it will be you. Twenty-four hours a day, 365 days a year, an average of 120 persons each hour are murdered or raped, physically assaulted or robbed with a deadly weapon.[6] An army of criminal offenders is responsible for bringing disaster to an estimated 3 to 5 million people in 1977. Spread over a year's time and scattered over the country, the millions of casualties of violent crime are not as noticeable as a few hundred victims of a flood in a single town. Though crime injures greater numbers of people than do natural disasters, its victims remain invisible.

If 3 to 5 million people were victims of any single natural disaster—earthquake, fire, or flood—the entire nation would react immediately. Under those circumstances collective action is spontaneously organized. But violent crimes are inflicted on one individual at a time in thousands of scattered events over the nation. Even though there are more casualties due to violent crimes with a greater number of deaths and seriously injured each year than casualties caused by natural disasters, they are less visible and less concentrated, thus making it more difficult for a collective response to be made. Furthermore, the danger of being a victim of a violent crime is continuous, persistent, and widespread, while a natural disaster that endangers people in a relatively small and defined area is episodic, and of relatively short duration.

The "disaster" character of violent crime is evidenced by the fact that there were an average of 1,440 victims of aggravated assault, 1,108 victims of violent robbery, 180 victims of forcible rape, and 53 men and women murdered every twenty-four hours in the United States in 1977[7]. These are based on official figures from the FBI Uniform Crime Report. Since a number of studies[8] have found that the true crime rate is approximately double that reported by the FBI, the extent of the crime disaster is probably twice that cited above.

The federal government has given aid to victims of fire, flood, earthquakes, tornadoes, and even grasshopper ravages since

1827. Every idea has its time. The time for Congress to recognize the need of federal aid for victims of violent crime is already here. The idea of giving the same consideration to victims of violent crime as to victims of a natural disaster may seem farfetched. But the blackout in New York City in July 1977 proved that disaster status for high-crime areas is realistic and possible.

On the evening of July 18, 1977 a vast power failure plunged New York City and Westchester County into darkness. The power failed at 9:34 P.M., apparently when lightning struck a Consolidated Edison electrical transmission line. The blackout triggered an unprecedented wave of looting which lasted through the night and well into the morning hours. Almost as soon as the lights went out the police were flooded with reports of muggings, pocketbook snatchings, and numerous break-ins at stores. Before the sun rose, gunfire crackled in many neighborhoods with the police reporting they were under sniper fire.[9]

Even as Mayor Beame was decrying "a night of terror" at a noontime City Hall news conference, roving bands of youths and adults were breaking into stores, carrying off food, furniture and television sets. The Mayor said that he had been in touch with court officials and had been assured they will be punished. . . .

At Mayor Beame's request, Governor Carey also asked the Disaster Assistance Administration to provide emergency relief for the small merchants whose businesses were destroyed by the disorders.[10]

Most of the city, state, and federal politicians were caught up in the game of making public statements advocating policies that would be politically expedient for their careers, but none of them publicly voiced the real issue. Everyone was willing to aid the businessman. The Small Business Administration reacted with speed thought impossible of the torturously slow bureaucracies of Washington, conferring "disaster aid" status on New York and Westchester. However, the individual victim, made destitute by mugging or having a purse stolen or apartment burned out, was denied the assistance available under the Federal Disaster Assistance Act, for President Carter refused to declare the city a disaster area under the act because the blackout was not a "natural disaster" and thus did not qualify.

By its actions the government acknowledged that "disaster"

status is legitimate and available for small businessmen who are victims of crime. Disaster status, however, is not legitimate and available for individual victims who do not own a business. The issue is no longer whether "disaster status" is legitimate for victims of crime, but whether it is to be reserved only for businessmen—who mainly suffer loss of business property—and denied to individual victims who suffer personal violence as well as loss of personal property.

Disaster status for the individual victim of violent crime in exceptionally high crime areas is the basic policy issue emerging from the aftermath of the blackout. "Disaster status" for the inhabitants of high-crime areas would bring the much-needed emergency aid that individual victims who personally suffer violent crime so desperately need.

The government has created an extensive disaster relief program that mobilizes the resources of federal, state, and local public agencies, as well as numerous private agencies, to bring aid and assistance to the victims of natural disasters. In 1975 the Federal Disaster Assistance Administration (FDAA), the government agency responsible for assisting disaster victims, provided $5.5 million through the Department of Labor to persons who were unemployed due to a natural disaster.[11] There is no federal provision for financial assistance to persons unemployed due to a violent crime.

In the same year more than 20,000 individual and family grants were made to those who were otherwise unable to cover costs of serious disaster-related needs. A typical grant was for $1,500 and was used to repair a home, replace furniture and appliances, replace clothing, or pay medical and funeral expenses. Victims of violent crimes, with the same needs, received no such federal aid.[12]

Approximately 11,600 families whose housing was made uninhabitable or inaccessible due to natural disasters in 1975 were provided with suitable temporary housing in the form of government-owned or rented units, mobile homes, prefabricated dwellings, or rapid repairs to their own homes. The FDAA authorizes assistance in the form of mortgage or rental payments for up to one year for disaster victims.[13] No such assistance is available to victims of violent crimes.

A total of nearly $79 million was given to individuals or families victimized by natural disasters in 1975. Loans to small businessmen and farmers affected by natural disasters amounted to $110 million.[14] In contrast, there are no federal aid or loan programs for individual victims of violent crimes.

To deal with a natural disaster, the government mobilizes every resource at the city, state, and federal level, as well as volunteer organizations, to help individual victims and restore the community to normal functioning as rapidly as possible. Society's response is immediate because the social structure is disrupted and the normal economic and social functions of the community cannot be carried on. Natural disasters drastically affect a community, threatening economic collapse and widespread social disorganization. Emergency disaster aid is necessary to restore community functioning as quickly as possible so that its social and economic life supports its inhabitants. Disaster measures are rendered without question of entitlements, deservedness, or prejudice. No one is concerned about the few who might feign injury or loss to secure benefits—they are inconsequential in the face of the vast problem of restoring the community to normal functioning.

The human response to natural disaster is often heroic. Volunteers rush to rescue complete strangers. People risk their own lives to assist those in immediate danger. Many people mobilize within themselves unusual courage and stamina.

Societies survive because people have learned that the struggle against nature requires the concentrated cooperation and organization of human activity. A natural disaster strikes indiscriminately, threatens all individuals within its scope, and cannot be prevented or effectively controlled by selected individuals. It therefore arouses the deepest survival instincts of cooperation and organization. Groups of people spontaneously organize for effective assistance. Because the danger comes from outside the social system, there is a general feeling of camaraderie, of "we are all in this together" that stimulates a desire to be helpful. But an unmentioned social attitude exists that it is unwise, even foolish, to help a victim of a violent crime. Most people turn away and pretend nothing has happened to the victim of rape or mugging. That is why rape counselors, for example, lecturing women on how to prevent rape, instruct them to yell "fire" rather than "help" or "rape" if ever they are faced with the situation.

What accounts for this difference in society's attitude toward victims of natural disasters and those of man-made disasters? One important factor seems to be whether society's economic functions are disrupted. If they are, then a disaster is acknowledged and extraordinary aid is invoked. But if the economic functions of a community continue to operate, then crises suffered by even a very large number of victims and their families are considered isolated incidents of personal troubles—no matter how tragic.

The public has a general attitude that becoming a victim of a violent crime is part of the victim's normal pattern of existence. Most people consider individuals who suffer the disastrous effects of violent crimes as unfortunate victims of their own life style. They are thought unlucky and are promptly forgotten. In most natural disasters people are usually blameless—and helpless to stop them. Humanity's impotence to avert a natural disaster produces a fatalistic attitude toward the *cause* of such disaster and heroic responsiveness to its *effect* on men and women. Averting or minimizing the disaster by placing the responsibility on someone or something else is futile.

But when it is possible to blame someone or something for the holocaust, that attitude is reversed. Once blaming begins, people fix their attention on the *cause* of a disaster and become indifferent, often fatalistic, to the *effect* on its victims.

THE INVISIBLE VICTIM

This is a curious phenomenon in victim psychology. If catastrophe strikes beyond human responsibility and control, it tends to produce compassionate and often heroic behavior toward victims. But if responsibility or blame can be placed, then people behave as if aid to the victim is solely a matter of the perpetrator making amends. The victim's need for compassion and aid are considered the exclusive responsibility of the blamed. Not until they become victims themselves do people realize the suffering caused by this neglectful and unjust attitude. Behind placing the blame on the victim is an unspoken message: "If no one can be found to be blamed for your misfortune, you are deserving of all the help it is in our power to give you. But if your misfortune can be blamed on someone, the extent of our responsibility is to hold him accountable for your tragedy. We can do nothing else for you."

Once blame has been established, the victim is not only ignored but often is himself assigned a share of the blame. This tendency to blame the victim is not unlike that attitude existing for centuries which blames the poor for their own poverty and categorizes them as "undeserving." In the same way a victim of violent crime is often blamed or accused of provoking the crime or contributing in some way to his or her own victimization and characterized as "undeserving."

The literature on crime written by well-meaning but offender-oriented professionals is full of such shallow and illogical statements as the following by Mannheim:[15]

> [T]he distinction between criminal and victim, which in the former days appeared as clear as black and white, actually often becomes vague and blurred in individual cases. The longer and the more deeply the actions of the persons involved are scrutinized, the more doubtful will it occasionally be who is blamed for the tragic outcome.

Much is made by these criminologists of the concept of the victim precipitation or provocation. When both the victim and the offender have a history of criminal behavior, it may be difficult to determine who is the victim and who is the offender. But in

The Invisible Disaster

most cases the victim is an *innocent* victim even though he or she may have been careless, negligent, or even provocative. I do not share the view that carelessness, negligence, or even provocation on the part of the victim casts doubt on the guilt of the perpetrator or earns the victim a share of the blame. In forcible rape cases, for example, the victim is blamed if she has had previous sexual relations with someone else by consent or if she dresses in a sexually attractive manner. Unless she is a virgin, dresses plainly, and does not try to look attractive, she is very likely to be accused of precipitating or provoking the crime, and therefore she "shares the blame" for its occurrence.

NEWS ITEM[16]

Judge in Wisconsin Calls Rape by Boy "Normal Reaction"

Madison, Wis., May 26 (UPI)

When a 15-year-old boy raped a girl in a stairwell at West High School, Judge Archie Simonson ruled yesterday, he was reacting "normally" to prevalent sexual permissiveness and women's provocative clothing.

The judge decreed that this youth, who was found delinquent, should be permitted to stay at home under court supervision rather than placed in an institution or other rehabilitation center....

In his ruling, Judge Simonson mentioned newspaper advertisements, prostitution arrests, sex stories, several bars with nude dancing and young women who appear in public and "even in court" wearing revealing clothing.

"This community is well-known to be sexually permissive," he said. "Should we punish a 15- or 16-year-old boy who reacts to it normally?" ...

Judge Simonson said a year of court supervision would best serve the boy and the public. He ordered the youth to continue treatment through a youth program and to study at home with a public school teacher until he was reaccepted in school.

Responsible people do not take criminal advantage of others' carelessness or negligence, or allow themselves to be provoked into criminal violence. That some people do is no reason for rewarding such behavior or reducing the blame. Reducing blame

13

serves only to encourage criminal behavior. The attitude that people who suffer misfortune have only themselves to blame—the poor, the minorities, the victims of society, and the victims of crime—is not limited to professional criminologists, sociologists, and psychologists but exists generally. The whole concept of precipitation and provocation as legitimate excuses for attenuating responsibility for violent criminal acts is false, illogical, psychologically harmful to victims, and socially irresponsible. Blaming the victim is a common cause of the indifference toward victims of violent crime.

The alcoholic, the drug addict, the mentally ill, and the offender are "human disasters." They, like victims of natural disasters, have special status, and many millions in aid are dispensed to them. What characterizes these groups is the threat they pose to society—that is what gives them a high priority for public funds. Victims are not a threat to anyone, so no one knows or cares about them.

Some people argue that federal aid for victims of violent crime is too "welfare state-ish" or "socialistic." For many years the same arguments were made in response to the disaster of widespread unemployment. While the federal government has supplied aid to victims of natural disasters since 1827, efforts to provide federal aid for the unemployed during the depressions of 1893, 1914, and 1921 failed in Congress. It was not until the disastrous depression of 1929 that Congress finally recognized the legitimacy of federal aid to the unemployed. The time for Congress to recognize the need of federal aid for crime victims is here.

Some argue that it is a matter for the states or local municipalities to handle rather than the federal government. At the present time, twenty states have legislation creating Crime Victims Compensation Boards. These are inadequately financed, fouled by Catch-22 rules—token programs that help less than 1 percent of the victims of violent crime. Any adequate program, without federal aid, would impose a heavy financial burden on the states or local municipalities. Chapter 7 proposes a model crime victims' bill, and chapter 8 suggests a viable federal program of disaster aid to victims of violent crime.

If the public develops a more concerned attitude about victims, state and federal politicians will respond to a strong demand for victim aid programs. The legislation that already exists in twenty states is something to start with. On the federal level, Congressman Peter W. Rodino, Jr., of New Jersey has introduced a bill[17] to partially reimburse states that have victim compensation legislation. If it passes, we can expect that most states will enact some form of such legislation. However, it will take a strong surge of public support for the bill to pass both houses of Congress. Without it, the outcome is doubtful.

The balance on the scale of justice is out of kilter. Heavily weighted on the side of the offender, it lacks substance on the side of the victim. The struggle for offender justice is important. It cannot be allowed to lapse. But criminal justice is—or ought to be—the servant of social justice. And social justice is more than justice for only the criminal. Substantive legal and criminal justice procedures that assure the victim of social justice are needed now, to balance the system. A criminal justice system that dispenses justice to the criminal only is archaic.

A new perspective is necessary, one that views the victim as well as the state as the aggrieved party; protects victim citizens against the catastrophe of post-crime victimization; and recognizes the right of victims to a fair share of social justice.

Society owes compensation to victims because of its failure to protect them. But we do not have to justify recognizing the victim of a crime as a human disaster on the basis of social failure. Whether people are in need through their own fault, through some failure of society, or through some act of nature should be irrelevant. Shall we refuse food and shelter to the hungry and homeless because we are not to blame for their situation? Our humanitarian impulses deny such a philosophy. Victims of violent crime are as deserving of our compassion and aid as are any victims of a catastrophe, natural or man-made. It would never occur to us to ask if the victims of a natural disaster have earned emergency and restitutive aid. Every citizen has that right. I believe that violent crime victims are disaster victims and have a right to a special status. *Social justice requires that society take responsibility for making the victim whole again. Emergency financial assistance, medical care, legal services, and justice are the rights of every victim and the moral obligation of society.*

CHAPTER 2

FBI CRIME STATISTICS: A VICTIM'S PERSPECTIVE

NEWS ITEM[1]

Justice Dept. May Create New
Crime-Report Agency

Washington, April 19 (UPI)

The Justice Department plans to create a neutral agency to take over the F.B.I.'s crime reports and statistical work to make sure that the figures are more credible and are put to better use.

Deputy Attorney General Harold R. Tyler, Jr.—the No. 2 man in the Justice Department—has said that the information gathering costs too much and is often "partisan," and the data are often unavailable when needed for making decisions.

The Los Angeles Times reported that Mr. Tyler wanted to place the crime reports and other statistics in a central bureau that would have "no ax of its own to grind."

He has not singled out the F.B.I. in commenting about "partisan" information, but its annual uniform crime reports, based on police reports, have been accused of being susceptible to bias and election-year politics.

Mr. Tyler said an act of Congress was needed before the neutral agency could be created.

Each year the FBI issues the Uniform Crime Report (UCR), which presents their nationwide view of crime based on statistics

17

by city, county, and state law enforcement agencies. These statistics, shocking as they are, do not reveal the true picture of crime in the U.S. Crime statistics, like any other data, can be reported in a manner that conceals more than it reveals. The FBI report distorts the true crime rate, misleads the public about the number of victims, and covers up significant failures of the criminal justice system.

The discussion in this chapter is based on the Uniform Crime Report (UCR) issued by the FBI for the year 1976.[2] Because I am concerned only with victims of violent crime, I will not discuss victimless crimes such as gambling and prostitution or crimes of property such as burglary, larceny, and theft.

The Crime Index Categories for violent crime are defined by the FBI as follows:

1. *Murder and Nonnegligent Manslaughter*
   This crime index offense is defined as the willful killing of another. Deaths caused by negligence, suicide, accident, or justifiable homicide are not included in the count for this offense classification. Attempts to murder or assaults to murder are recorded as aggravated assaults and not as murder.[3]

2. *Aggravated Assault*
   Aggravated assault is defined as an unlawful attack by one person upon another for the purpose of inflicting severe bodily injury usually accompanied by the use of a weapon or means likely to produce death or serious bodily harm. Attempts are included since it is not necessary that an injury result when a gun, knife, or other weapon is used which could and probably would result in serious personal injury if the crime were successfully completed.[4]

3. *Forcible Rape*
   Forcible rape is the carnal knowledge of a female through the use of force or threat of force. Assaults to commit forcible rape are also included; however, statutory rape (without force) is not counted in this category.[5]

4. *Robbery*
   Robbery is a vicious type of crime which takes place in the presence of the victim to obtain property, or a thing of value from a person by use of force or threat of force. Assault to commit robbery and attempts are included. This is a violent crime which frequently results in injury to the victim.[6]

FBI Crime Statistics: A Victim's Perspective

Over *10 million* crimes were reported in the U.S. in 1976. Nearly 1 million of these, 986,580, were violent crimes. The national rate for violent crime calculated from these figures is given as 459.6 per 100,000 population. In 1976 there were nearly 5 reported violent crimes for every 1,000 citizens.

The figures given in the UCR are based on offenses in the records of thousands of law enforcement agencies, reported on a monthly basis. The report frankly admits that it does not know the true total volume of crime.

A considerable gap exists between the number of crimes reported by the police and those that actually occur. This gap has been called the "dark figure"[7] of crime, and its existence severely limits the validity of crime statistics in the United States. Among the many factors contributing to this "dark figure" are bad information processing; distortions, even outright falsification; discretionary practices of the police, modifying or altering the charge; and last but not least, the failure of the victim to report the crime.

Precinct captains are often under pressure to falsify crime statistics to take the heat off their supervisors. A high police department official of a large city commented, "The unwritten law was that you were supposed to make things look good. You weren't supposed to report all the crime that actually took place in your precinct—and, if you did, it could be your neck. I know captains who actually lost their commands because they turned in honest crime reports."[8]

FBI instructions to the police on information processing leads to considerable underreporting. When more than one kind of crime is committed by an offender, the FBI asks the police to report to the UCR only the "most serious" criminal act.

If, for example, an offender commits forcible rape, burglarizes the house, physically assaults the victim, and steals the victim's automobile, only the forcible rape is to be reported by the police to the FBI. The amount of physical harm or the loss or damage to property is therefore not counted as such, and many acts are not recorded statistically.[9]

Multiple crimes on a victim thus appear in the UCR as the single "most serious" crime, resulting in a reduction in the true crime picture.

Although the popular belief is that police have little discretion in their work, in actuality they have considerable discretion and use it constantly. The police will often charge an offender with a misdemeanor when a felony has been committed. Sometimes the police are aware that an offender has committed a number of offenses—the offender may have even admitted them during questioning—but rather than bothering to gather evidence to substantiate all the admitted offenses, the police charge him with the one offense they believe can be made to stick.

These practices often cause victims to feel frustrated and disbelieving. They cannot understand how the catastrophe they have suffered could be ignored simply because the police find it more convenient to charge the offender with a different crime (sometimes a lesser crime) against another person.

Here is an excerpt from a case file of a counselor of the Crime Victims Service Center in the Bronx, New York.

Mrs. O's husband went outside to fix his car and was never seen by her again. A man who killed two women was found with Mr. O's car. He admitted killing him, throwing the body in a garbage bin which was later dumped under 65,000 tons of garbage. The police said since it was too expensive to dig for the body, they have no habeas corpus. When Mrs. O found out about her husband she had a heart attack. Mrs. O is under doctor's care. There has been no funeral expenses because there is no body. Her main concern is that the criminal be convicted. I called up the ——— Homicide Zone and was told that the criminal will never be tried for this crime because there is no body.[10]

By their decision the police have prevented Mrs. O from providing a decent burial for her slain husband and deprived her of any victim's benefits to which she might be entitled.

The greatest distortion of the true crime rate stems from the failure to report the crime—particularly violent crime. Crimes such as felonious assault and homicide are called "personal" crimes because they bring the victim face-to-face with the offender. Personal crimes frequently involve members of the same family or acquaintances from the same neighborhood or work group as the victim, and this fact often accounts for the victim's reluctance to cooperate with the police, press charges, or become a witness.

I have already commented on the degree of terror to which victims are subjected. They cannot be certain they are safe even if the offender is jailed. Victims have learned by experience to have little confidence in the ability or willingness of the police to protect them. In these circumstances it may be foolhardy to report the crime to the police.

Some victims of felonious assault constitute a special type I call the victim-offender. In a bar brawl, for example, who becomes the victim and who the offender is frequently accidental. The one who draws the knife first or who inflicts the greatest injury is considered the offender. The victim may have been an offender in a previous altercation. The victim-offender is less willing to report the crime, press charges, become a witness, or seek help of any kind.

Another reason for the high rate of unreported crime lies in the life style of most victims. The high-crime areas of the nation are where the poor and the aged live. Their lives are daily victimizations by landlords, merchants, and bureaucratic service organizations. Victimization is the normal pattern of existence to be endured. Bitter experience has taught them that to complain is often costly and frequently places them in jeopardy or causes them to be blamed or held responsible. Under these circumstances reporting a crime is a futile and sometimes degrading experience. For all of these reasons the FBI reports are distorted.

What then is the true crime rate? The staff of the National Commission on the Causes and Prevention of Crime attempted to find out the extent of unreported crime. Their surveys estimated the true crime rate for rape to be three and one-half times greater than that reported by the FBI, the rate of aggravated assault, two times greater than reported by the FBI, and one and one-half times higher than reported for robbery.[11] The consensus among investigators is that the true crime rate is double the rate reported in the UCR. The true violent crime rate for 1976, therefore, is probably close to 2 million.

Can we assume there were 2 million *victims* of violent crime in 1976? By no means. The statement in the UCR that "a crime rate may be viewed as a victim risk rate"[12] is based on the false assumption there is only one victim for each crime. But when the head of a household is murdered, the entire family becomes a victim. If a wage earner suffers serious physical injury and the loss of earning potential, the entire family is victimized. Often more than one person, including bystanders, are injured in a single crime. The UCR crime rates are based on the number of reported *offenses*; these do not give a true picture of the number of *victims*. A single offense may result in 1 to 6 victims. A conservative estimate of 2 victims per offense based on a true crime rate of 2 million suggests between 3 and 5 million victims of violent crime in 1976.

These estimates tell a story different from that of the FBI report. The UCR gives the impression of much less crime and fewer victims. It covers up the failure of law enforcement agencies to bring justice to most of the 3 to 5 million victims of violent crime. The UCR also gives the impression of a greater number of crimes solved, and a larger proportion of prosecutions and convictions, than the facts justify. I will demonstrate these distortions using the data in the UCR for 1976.

Arrests

The FBI reports the number of offenses in each violent crime category "cleared" or "solved" by arrests. Because an arrest is made, the offense is recorded as solved even though the arrested person may never be brought to trial or, if tried, may not be found guilty.

Here is an example of how the FBI reports "Persons Arrested" for murder.

Based on reports submitted by law enforcement agencies, 9 percent of all persons arrested [no figure given] for murder were under 18 years of age and 43 percent were under 25. During the period 1972–1976, there was a 27 percent decrease in the number of persons under 17 years of age arrested for murder. The adult arrests [no figure given] increased 13 percent for murder offenses during this period. Numerically, the 18 to 22 year age group had the heaviest involvement during 1976 with 24 percent of the total arrests [whatever that mysterious figure is] coming from this age group. Negroes made up 53 percent of the arrests for murder in 1976.[13]

You would be hard pressed to find a better example of statistical obfuscation than the preceding paragraph. I defy anyone to interpret the significance of these percentages without knowing the number of arrests made—a figure that appears to be deliberately withheld. How many arrests for murder does an increase of 13 percent represent—200, 2,000, or 10,000? Without knowing how many were arrested, it is impossible to evaluate the meaning of these percentages.

Prosecutions

Reporting prosecutions, the statistical counting unit changes. Whereas arrests are reported in terms of a percentage of offenses, prosecutions are reported in terms of a percentage of arrests. How many *crimes* are accounted for by prosecutions is not reported, and without knowing the number of arrests—only percentages are given—it is impossible to calculate. After considerable searching I finally found a table that reported the number of arrests in each crime index. From this I calculated the number of offenses accounted for by prosecutions.[14] The effect of this shift in the statistical counting unit is to give the impression of a higher percentage of prosecutions.

The quantity of arrested offenders brought to trial provides useful information about the efficiency of the police in making a proper arrest and gathering evidence to make prosecution possible. But prosecutions also are—or ought to be—an indication of how many crimes they account for. For example, if 90 percent of those arrested are prosecuted, we would say the police ars doing a good job of making arrests that can stand up to the rigors of prosecution. But if only 10 percent of crimes resulted in arrest, then the 90 percent prosecution-to-arrest rate actually signifies that only 9 percent of crimes committed result in prosecution. We would have to conclude that the police are doing a poor job of law enforcement. The FBI reports only the former. Both the percentage of those arrested who are prosecuted and the percentage of crimes committed and resulting in prosecution are important. To report only the former is to give an exaggerated account of the "success" of law enforcement agencies.

Convictions

The philosophy of our offender-oriented criminal justice system is based on the concept of punishment as a deterrent. Until recently the rationale that *fear* of punishment would act as a constraint on those inclined to engage in criminal activities dominated criminal justice policy. Lately a growing view that not fear but *certainty* of punishment acts as a constraint has become fashionable in criminal justice circles. From this new viewpoint it is especially important to know how many crimes actually result in convictions. Here, too, though the FBI has the information, it does not report it. What it does report about convictions gives a false and inflated impression of the success of the criminal justice system.

One may calculate a conviction rate in two ways. One method is to calculate, as the FBI does, the percentage of those cases brought to trial that result in conviction. In the Crime Index category of rape, for example, the report says, "Forty-two percent of the adults prosecuted were found guilty of the substantive offense and 9 percent were convicted of lesser offenses,"[15] making a total of 51 percent of adult prosecutions resulting in convictions. This gives us information only about the probability of conviction *if the offender is brought to trial*. In addition to reporting the conviction rate of only those who have been arrested and tried, significant information could be provided by reporting the rate of conviction *for the total number of rapes*. A conviction rate of 51 percent of those arrested and tried gives a misleading impression if only 11 percent of those who commit rape are convicted.

Murder

The FBI claims, "Nationally, police continue to be successful in clearing or solving by arrest a greater percentage of homicides than any other Crime Index offense. In 1976, 79 percent of the homicides were solved; and in 1975, 78 percent of all murder offenses were solved."[16] The impression is given that the police in 1976 successfully established who the murderer was in 79 percent of the killings. Reading on you will find that "71 percent of all adults arrested for murder in 1976 were prosecuted during the year. Forty-eight percent of the adults prosecuted were found guilty as charged, and 14 percent were convicted on some lesser charge."[17]

Although the narrative does not inform us how many persons

were arrested, it states that 7 percent of those arrested were juveniles and that 71 percent of the adults arrested were prosecuted. We are not told how *many* adults were prosecuted. A true percentage of the number of murders resulting in adult prosecutions and conviction is impossible to calculate from these figures. Again we must refer to the table on the number of arrests and calculate the results ourselves.

On this basis calculations show that out of 18,780 reported killings, 14,836 (79 percent) were "cleared" by the arrest of 14,113 persons. Seven percent of these (988) were juveniles, leaving 13,125 adults arrested. There were 9,319 adult prosecutions resulting from 18,780 reported murders. Approximately 50 percent of the murders resulted in prosecutions. Calculations further show that 24 percent of murders resulted in a murder conviction and 7 percent resulted in a conviction on a lesser charge.

The statement that 71 percent of adults arrested were prosecuted gives the impression that a higher number of prosecutions took place than is actually the case. In actuality, only 50 percent of the murders reported resulted in adults prosecuted. This picture of murder statistics is totally different from the impression given by the FBI report that 79 percent of homicides were solved. Stated simply, the figures tell us that while an arrest was made in 79 percent of the reported cases of murder, *at least 69 percent of the murders were unpunished*—a fact that raises some critical questions about the effectiveness of the entire criminal justice system.

Aggravated Assault

In 1976, 490,854 aggravated assaults were reported. The FBI reports that 64 percent of these cases were cleared by arrests. Seventy percent of adults arrested were prosecuted. Convictions were handed down in 46 percent of the prosecutions, 13 percent of which were for a lesser charge.

Recalculating these percentages in terms of the number of offenses accounted for, we find 23 percent of offenses led to prosecutions; only 9 percent of reported aggravated assaults resulted in conviction as charged, and 3 percent ended with a conviction on a lesser charge.

Rape

In 1976, 56,730 rapes were reported. According to the UCR 52 percent were cleared by arrests. Sixty-nine percent of adults arrested were prosecuted; 42 percent of adults prosecuted were found guilty of the substantive offense, and 9 percent were convicted of lesser offenses.

In terms of offenses, these figures mean that 21 percent of rape offenses resulted in adults prosecuted, 9 percent of rapes ended with adults convicted as charged, and 2 percent were accounted for by adults convicted on a lesser charge.

Robbery

The report informs us there were 420,210 robbery offenses in 1976. Twenty-seven percent of the offenses were cleared by arrests. This does not mean that that many persons were arrested. Actually, 76,104 adults and 34,192 juveniles were arrested. According to the report 72 percent of the adults arrested were prosecuted. Calculations reveal that of the 420,210 robbery offenses reported, only 13 percent led to adults being prosecuted. That's a long way from the impression given by the UCR figure of a 72-percent prosecution rate. That percentage is not inaccurate. It is simply misleading.

When it comes to convictions, the UCR is just as misleading. It reports that 56 percent of those prosecuted were found guilty as charged, and 8 percent were found guilty of a lesser charge. Calculating the number of offenses accounted for by convictions, we find that in 1976 only 10 percent of robberies resulted in convictions and 1 percent of robberies resulted in conviction on a lesser charge.

The following table shows the difference between the percentages of adults prosecuted and convicted for each violent crime reported in the UCR and the ratio of prosecutions and convictions of adults to the number of crimes committed (figures for juveniles are not available).

Adults Prosecuted

Crime Index Category	% Reported by FBI	Calculated % of Offenses
Murder	71	50
Aggravated Assault	70	23
Rape	69	21
Robbery	72	13

Adults Convicted*

Murder	62	31
Aggravated Assault	54	12
Rape	51	11
Robbery	64	18

* Includes those convicted of the substantive charge or a lesser one.

Thus in 1976 the chances of an adult offender going unpunished for each type of violent crime was:

Murder	69 out of 100
Aggravated Assault	88 out of 100
Rape	89 out of 100
Robbery	92 out of 100

FBI Crime Statistics: A Victim's Perspective

If it is true that the certainty of punishment is an important factor in deterring violent criminal activity, then the criminal justice system fails miserably to provide that constraint.

If we take all reported violent crimes of 1976 and all adults convicted for each violent crime index in that year, we find that an average of 15.5 percent of all violent crimes resulted in convictions. An average of 84.5 of each 100 adult perpetrators of violent crimes escaped without punishment.

Remember, these percentages are calculated on the basis of *reported* crimes. If they were calculated on the estimated true crime rate of double that reported by the FBI, the average conviction rate would be less than 8 percent.[18] Thus, an average of 92 out of 100 perpetrators of violent crime in 1976 went unpunished. From the perspective of the 3 to 5 million victims each year, more than 92 out of 100 found no solace in the workings of the criminal justice system. To speak of justice to them is a farce.

No information is available about the degree of seriousness of the physical and economic harm suffered by individual victims of violent crime. It is important to know how frequent and widespread is the senseless and vicious brutality with which some offenders treat helpless and defenseless victims. More important, I believe that offenders who commit such atrocities should be treated differently from those who commit the same legally defined crime but with less serious violence, even though the law's definition of the seriousness of the crime is the same.

It is important to know whether people are getting more violent. By this I mean not whether more people are becoming violent, but rather whether criminals are becoming less restrained in their violent behavior. Does our culture today legitimate forms of violent behavior that would formerly have been too reprehensible even for a criminal? How widespread among offenders is senseless, sadistic behavior?

Even the police, to whom sadism is everyday stuff, are puzzled by the senseless violence that often accompanies the robbery of old people. Are criminals becoming more violent? If so, why? No data is available to answer these serious questions.

The necessity for data on "seriousness" was suggested as early as 1969 in the staff report to the National Commission on the Causes and Preventions of Violence. The staff points out:

> There is no weighting by seriousness of offense when the [UCR] index is considered as a whole. There is no difference in seriousness, for example, between a $50.00 larceny and a premeditated murder. Each offense represents a unit of one in the crime index total volume (and the crime index rate computed from it and population totals). Because there are many more property crimes than violent crimes the index is greatly overweighted towards property offenses. It is consequently possible, for example, that a marked decline in those violent crimes generally assumed most serious—criminal homicide and forcible rape—could be offset by minor increases in property crimes.[19]

Under these circumstances, the total number of crimes on the Crime Index represents an invalid, inaccurate measure of the amount and quality of criminality in a community.

One cannot use a simple mathematical scale to measure the loss a victim suffers. A loss of fifty dollars or an injury requiring hospitalization does not represent the same loss to a family earning $15,000 a year as it does to a family in the $3,000-a-year bracket. To a person in the lower socioeconomic bracket, the loss of fifty dollars represents the loss of 2 percent of the annual income. It can make the difference between being able or unable to pay rent or utility bills. An injury requiring hospitalization puts an added burden on the lower-income person, who probably is already a medical indigent.

The groundwork has already been laid for an index that accurately reflects the seriousness of the crime it reports. Although almost ten years ago the task force recommended that the UCR should give top priority to this matter, nothing has been done. To this day, there is little or no collection of criminal statistics indicating the amount of harm, suffering, loss to the community or to the victims of violent crime. I will return to the matter of the measure of seriousness later when I discuss how we might measure a disaster area.

Awareness of the misleading nature of the UCR has prompted some efforts at gathering *victim* statistics. More than ten years ago, the crime commission undertook the first of a number of victim surveys. A sample of the population was interviewed and asked if, when, and how it had been victimized. One of these surveys undertaken by the National Opinion Research Center (NORC) at the University of Chicago indicated that the 1965 victim rate for the four violent crimes was more than double the comparative UCR rate for individuals.[20] The NORC rate was three and a half times greater than the UCR rate for forcible rape, one and a half times the UCR robbery rate, and twice the aggravated assault rate. In three Washington, D.C., precinct studies, the estimated victim rate was more than four times as high as the police rate.

The Law Enforcement Assistance Administration (LEAA) has commissioned a number of victim studies. Most of them indicate the number of victims to be at least double that of the UCR rate. According to LEAA, its national crime survey program is designed to develop information not otherwise available on the nature of crime and its impact on society, by means of victimization studies of the general population.

LEAA recognizes, however, that "victimization surveys such as those conducted under the National Crime Survey Program are not without limitations."[21]

Recognizing that surveys are most successful with specific victims who understand what happened to them, how it happened, and who are willing to report what they know, LEAA has focused on those crimes where these conditions appear most applicable. Murder and kidnapping are not covered.

Surveys, in general, have several limitations. The success of any survey depends, to a large degree, on the respondents' willingness to cooperate. Since surveys of victims are retrospective, they are subject to distortions in the victim's recall of the incident. For example, one of the characteristics of memory recall is the tendency to telescope events. Thus, victims may report incidents outside the time frame of the survey or report effects of different events as a single event. LEAA has no objective data on the degree of willingness to cooperate or the degree of telescoping among victims.

Even more discouraging is the practice in the LEAA survey of counting a number of crimes as only one if they took place in a single criminal event. Should an offender rob a woman, beat her with a weapon, and then rape her, only the "most serious" crime—the rape—would be counted. Clearly, the LEAA surveys are still using the UCR concept of seriousness.

Several states have conducted their own victimization surveys. A Texas survey for 1975 reports a 17.5 percent victimization rate—slightly more than one out of six Texas citizens were victims in 1975. The UCR rate for 1975 indicates a crime rate of 8 percent—almost half of the victim rate in the Texas survey.[22]

A number of victim studies that appear to be counting the same thing give different results because their basis for counting is different. The FBI victim rate is based on a count of offenses per 100,000 population. The LEAA victim rate is based on victimization *incidents* per 1,000 population. Other surveys are based on a count of individual *victims* rather than incidents. Since each counts differently, it cannot be directly compared with another or with the UCR.

Almost all victimization studies are based on the survey method. A sample of the population is taken to estimate what victimization is like for the total population. Primarily, the studies focus on arriving at an estimate of the "true rate" of victimization for the population; the number of victimizations in each crime index category; victimizations relative to class category; and an indication of the relative risk of being victimized.

Victimization, like crime, is a class phenomenon. The lower the socioeconomic class, the greater the risk of becoming a victim of a violent crime. The 1975 Texas survey reported that all income groups over $15,000 had a below-average risk of violent crime. No one in the sample of the over-$50,000 income group was a victim of a violent crime.[23]

In the LEAA Victims Survey for 1974, the victimization rate for crimes of violence per 1,000 persons aged 12 and over for those with less than $3,000 annual family income was 54.3, more than double the rate for those in the $25,000 annual family income bracket. As the income bracket goes up, the victimization rate decreases. The victimization rate for the annual family income bracket of $25,000 and over was 25 percent. The same trends are visible in the 1975 victimization survey.[24] Contrary to middle-class fears of widespread "crime in the streets," the majority of the victims of violent crimes are the ghetto residents of the large metropolitan cities.

Victimization for property crimes, on the other hand, tends to increase with increases in the annual family income. The victimization rates for property crime such as theft and larceny are higher than for violent crimes in every income bracket from lowest to highest. And the victimization rate increases as the annual income bracket rises. The victimization for crimes of property (theft) for the lowest income bracket in 1974 was 80.7 per 1,000 persons aged 12 and older. For the highest income bracket ($25,000 and over) it was 127.7. Remember, however, that theft represents a more serious loss for the poor.[25]

Statistically, it is quite clear that the areas high in violent crime are those central cities of large metropolitan areas with high population density that are usually composed of one or more ghettos. For example, in 1974 the victimization rate for violent crime in metropolitan areas with central cities of from 500,000 to 1,000,000 population are as follows: Inside the central cities, the victimization rate for violent crimes was 48.9 per 1,000 aged 12 and over. The victimization rate for outside the central city areas was 37.5. In metropolitan cities with central city populations of a million or over, the victimization rate for inside the central city areas was 47.5; outside these central city areas the victimization rate was 38.0.

For crimes of property, the victimization rate for metropolitan areas with 500,000 to 1,000,000 population was 121.5 inside the central city areas and 122.5 outside the central city areas. In metropolitan areas with a population of a million or over, the rate for inside the central city areas was 86.5. The rate for outside the central city areas was 113.3[26]

Why collect data on crime victims at all? For what purpose should we seek information about victims?

LEAA claims that its national victim surveys generate a variety of data to provide the following information: (1) compute the relative risk of being victimized for identifiable sectors of society; (2) record the circumstances under which crimes occur and their effect; (3) estimate the cost of crime in terms of injury or economic loss; and (4) reveal why criminal acts are not reported to authorities.

But its promise is mere rhetoric. In its 179-page report,[27] there are no data offered, no information reported about the second, third, and fourth items. The entire report is devoted to data relevant to the first item. If LEAA has any data relevant to the last three items, it is a well-hidden secret. I suspect, however, that what data LEAA does have in these areas is so unreliable that it would be embarrassing to report it. In fact, the overriding purpose of the LEAA surveys appears to be to test the hypothesis (ad infinitum) of a discrepancy between the UCR reports and the true crime rate and to provide an estimate of the size of this gap. Like the other offender-oriented elements of the criminal justice system, LEAA's primary interest is in crime. Its surveys of victims produce data more relevant to the police than to the social evaluation of the victim problem.

To arrive at a deeper understanding of the social issue of victimization, we would need data such as: (1) the effect of crime on victims in terms of the degree of seriousness of the loss, including economic as well as physical and mental health loss. This should include data regarding the relative loss to each victim—for example, loss expressed in terms of percent of annual income; (2) the needs of victims of violent crimes (for detailed example, see chapter 3); (3) the special needs of the different types of victims (for example, the elderly); and (4) measures to help prevent victimization and revictimization.

Data such as this would provide information necessary for planning and evaluation of programs to assist victims and prevent victimization and revictimization. This type of information requires intimate knowledge of the victimization process and its effects. It can hardly be gotten from the one- or two-hour retrospective interviews with an ex-victim characteristic of present surveys. One must establish contact with the victim while he is still in the throes of the victimization process—as close to the time of the crime as possible—and follow him through every step in his efforts to recover from the trauma of the violent crime.

In 1973, my colleagues and I at the Center for the Study of Social Intervention of the Albert Einstein College of Medicine designed the first victim study in the United States that attempted to gather information about victims by actually operating a service for them. The following chapter describes this program and relates what we learned from the victims we serviced.

CHAPTER 3

A SERVICE
FOR VICTIMS

The Crime Victims Service Center was set up in the Bronx, New York, with the aim of securing for adult victims financial, medical, legal, and preventive services needed as a result of a violent crime. The purposes of operating this service was to gather data on the needs of violent crime victims in the Bronx; to study the issues in providing such services; and, as a result of this experience, to design a service for victims of violent crime for all of New York City. Careful attention was paid to documenting this project, for it was the first attempt at generating data about victims from a service rather than surveys.

Data was collected on 259 victims of violent crime in the Bronx during an eighteen-month period. Because the number of victims is small, the data cannot be extrapolated to all victims of violent crime, but the results can provide an insight into what it means to be a victim of a violent crime in a high-crime area in a metropolitan city; the needs of these victims; how the human service agencies respond to these needs; and how the victims respond to the human service agencies.

During the two-year study, we learned many important facts

about victims that few people are aware of—about their suffering, their frustration, and their hopelessness. We learned about the invisibility of the agony of victims of violent crime. Most shocking of all, we learned that the crime itself serves to launch the victim on a series of post-crime victimizations by the police, the courts, the human service agencies, and the federal government.

For reasons already discussed, victims of violence and their families do not rush to seek help or assistance. Often, only sheer desperation prompts them to make an effort to find help. The victims who came to the Crime Victims Service Center represented the most desperate in the Bronx.

Since the high-crime areas of the Bronx are also the neighborhoods of the poor and the disenfranchised, the victims seen were the economically and socially deprived people of the ghetto. Because our experience was with the poorest and most desperate of the victims, the conclusions may appear distorted and not applicable to most victims of violent crime. But studies have established that the majority of victims of violent crimes come from the poorest sectors of the large metropolitan cities of America.

These observations are limited by the fact that the Crime Victims Service Center did not serve all victims of crime but served only those of violent crime. It did not serve victims of crimes of property without violence, such as burglary, larceny, and so on. Throughout this book the victims I write about are the poor, those on welfare, those who are underemployed—working only a few days a week—and those full-time employees who earn less than $8,000 a year for a family of four. They live in high-crime ghetto areas of large metropolitan cities and constitute the majority of victims of violent crime. I am convinced, however, that much of what we learned can be extrapolated to most victims of violent crime regardless of their economic and social conditions.

The Crime Victims Service Center (CVSC)

The general mandate of this two-year program was to operate a crime victims' center in the Bronx to explore the most feasible and effective organization of services to meet the needs of victims. The population to be serviced were those crime victims upon whom some physical insult had been inflicted. This included the families of murder victims, victims of rape, felonious assault, and robbery with assault. The long-range objective was to assess the viability of a "victims' service" and recommend a citywide system suitable for delivering services to victims of violent crime.

This mandate was operationalized in two major undertakings. The first was a survey of the needs of 10,000 victims of crimes of violence throughout New York City, excepting those in the Bronx. The second, the heart of the project, was the development of a referral service for victims of violent crime in the Bronx.

Five paraprofessional counselors were trained as expediters and advocates to assist victims to meet whatever needs arose from their victimization. This action component of the project was designed to secure needed services for victims and at the same time to accumulate data about their needs, their utilization patterns, the best technique for making contact, and the viability of assisting victims by providing advocates to represent them before the various social welfare agencies. In addition, this action component was to serve as a check on the survey results by comparing the needs expressed by survey respondents—who were relying on retrospective memory to provide answers to an interviewer's questions—with the actions of those victims who were actually using services during a crisis.

I assumed major responsibility for the design of the program for delivery of services, including the development of a method for obtaining victim referrals from police precincts and the recruitment and training of the five crime victim advocates. David Friedman, then Project Coordinator and later Associate Director, assumed responsibility for compiling an inventory of social agencies and establishing liaison with local, city, state, federal, and private service agencies in order to establish procedures for securing services for victims. He assisted in the recruitment and training of the counselors and developed a manual of service resources for their use. He was also responsible for continuous weekly supervision of the counselors.

The selection, hiring, and intensive training of the service counselors (one Black male and female, one Hispanic male and female, and one White female) were completed by January 1974, at which time the service became operational.

Now, for the first time, a public-supported free service was available to all victims of violent crime in the Bronx aged eighteen and over. We prepared for a flood of calls for help. We decided not to advertise too widely because we did not want more cases than we could handle. We did not want to provoke the cynicism about public agencies that make people wait weeks for help they need immediately. We knew there were a large number of invisible victims in the community who needed our help, and we began to look for them.

Almost all the victim studies sponsored by LEAA prior to the CVSC addressed themselves to the victim-witness. The ostensible aim was to help the victim in the judicial process. Politically, the studies were motivated by the pressure of criminal justice administrators to relieve the backlog of court cases by speeding up trials through assistance to and education of the victim as witness.

Another reason for the focus on victim-witnesses was the relative ease of contacting them. All one had to do was to set up an office in the court building and contact witnesses as they appeared for hearings or trials. Also, by the time victims got to court, they had partially recovered from the trauma of the crime and were more able to help themselves and make better use of services.

From the outset of the service operation, we decided that it would be most desirable for us to make contact with the victim as close to the time of the crime as possible. At each step, from police action to court trial, victims get filtered out of the system. *Only 5 to 15 percent of the total victim population ever gets to court.* The needs of victims begin at the time of the crime; the closer to that we could make contact, the more effectively we could serve them.

If the Crime Victims Service Center limited itself to victim-witnesses, it would never have had the opportunity to observe and understand the degree of shock that victims often experienced. A program to assist victims cannot be considered effective if it is designed to service only 15 percent of the total number of victims.

We believed that if it were possible to make initial contact with each victim and offer him help at the time the crime occurred, the service could accomplish its goal of offering assistance to a more representative group of victims. We experimented with having counselors ride in police cars and contact the victims at the scene of the crime. But this turned out to be costly and ineffective. Too much time was spent riding around in the police car. And, when contact was made, often the victim was injured and needed immediate medical attention first, before any discussion or assessment of other help was possible. Consequently, we obtained permission from the Bronx Commander of Police, Anthony Bouza, for our counselors to visit the precincts and secure the names and addresses of victims of violent crimes that occurred during the previous twenty-four to forty-eight hours.

Those who had telephones were contacted by phone. The others were written a letter, either in English or Spanish, explaining our service, offering our help, and asking them to contact us by phone or in person, with no appointment necessary. If we did not hear from them in two weeks, a follow-up letter was sent. If no reply to our follow-up letter was received, the counselor made a home visit.

Our anticipation of a crowd of needy victims overwhelming us with demands for service was naive. We learned that *need* must be distinguished from *utilization*—there is a wide gap between what victims need and what they are willing and able to do to get their needs cared for. Suspicion and distrust were very high on the list of reasons for this gap. The idea of a victims' service was unheard of and aroused suspicion in the minds of victims, even those familiar with the usual services offered by the human service agencies. Some victims refused to talk to our counselors. They would call the police or the district attorney's office inquiring whether we were a legitimate agency. They suspected our offer was a trick of the offender or his accomplices. Victims who sought safety in anonymity, who were virtually in hiding in their homes, were panicked by the fact that some stranger had their name, address, and telephone number.

Securing the names of victims from the police put us in the position of being considered an arm of the police, or at least of having some fuzzy connection with them. From the outset, we were aware of this liability, but we felt we could overcome victims' reactions of suspicion and distrust, and that it would be worthwhile if getting the names from the police would enable us to reach a victim as quickly as possible after the occurrence of a crime.

Because of repeated experiences of callous indifference in human service agencies, some victims had a cynical attitude about our ability to help. Also, a general tendency among the poor in high-crime areas is to react with stoicism and a degree of acceptance of victimization as a condition of life. And among certain ethnic groups, people in need turn to their own families and friends rather than suffer what they consider to be a loss of dignity by turning to public service agencies.

Many of the victims had suffered serious injuries and were in the hospital or confined to bed at home for long periods. The crime often resulted in "shock," the victims isolating themselves out of fear and helplessness.

For all of these reasons, services tend to be utilized by that part of the victim population that has nowhere else to turn and whose needs are so great or so immediately vital that any reluctance to utilize a service is overcome.

Some victims needed considerable time to pull themselves together enough to make the effort to seek help. In spite of severe and urgent needs, it was rare for a victim of a violent crime to seek help immediately after the crime, except, of course, for medical assistance. How difficult it was for violent crime victims to try to get help is illustrated by the fact that even though efforts were made to contact victims within twenty-four to forty-eight hours of the crime, the first interview with a majority of those given services did not take place until *two to more than five weeks after the crime occurred*. Almost 30 percent were not interviewed until more than five weeks after the traumatic incident.

Newspaper and radio coverage about the Crime Victims Service Center did not create a surge in demand for services at the beginning of the project. Consequently, special outreach efforts were made to identify and contact individual crime victims in need of services. The magnitude and intensity of these outreach efforts are summarized as follows:

1. *Telephone:* Lists of crime victims were obtained from several police precincts in the service area of the Crime Victims Service Center. All those who had listed telephones were contacted by the counselors.
2. *Letters:* From those same precinct lists, all crime victims who had no telephones were sent letters notifying them of the service and offering help. These included persons whose telephone numbers turned out to be erroneous. Flyers describing the program in English and Spanish were included. Spanish letters were mailed to persons with Spanish surnames. A second letter was later com-

posed, and again the police precinct lists of victims were used for mail-outs.

3. *Newspaper articles* appeared in the *Daily News, New York Times, Bronx Press Review, Parkchester News, Co-op City News, Co-op City Times, El Diario,* and *El Tiempo.*

4. *Radio Programs:* Fordham University's community program was utilized for a half-hour presentation. Radio stations WHOM and WBNX presented two-minute spots in Spanish about the center for a two-month period, and WNBC presented a one-hour program on the center.

5. *Television:* The CVSC was given a one-minute spot commercial, which was presented by Channel 7 at intervals over a one-month period. Channel 41 presented a fifteen-minute and a five-minute program in Spanish.

6. *Pamphlets:* Approximately 5,000 copies of a pamphlet describing the CVSC's services were distributed to a variety of community agencies and groups.

7. *Posters:* Posters describing the Crime Victims Service Center were placed in stores, churches, and so on, and three hundred black-and-white posters, measuring 11 inches by 27 inches, were placed as institutional advertising in buses in the Bronx.

8. *Precinct Distribution:* Two thousand three-by-five cards, in both Spanish and English, were given to officers of the 48th Precinct for them to distribute to crime victims within that precinct.

9. *Agency and Community Group Visits:* In a two-month period, approximately 166 groups were approached by the counselors, and pamphlets were distributed for circulation by these agencies.

10. *Community Presentations:* Counselors attended forty-eight community meetings where they described the services of and answered questions about the Crime Victims Service Center.

11. *Direct Contact:* On seventeen separate occasions, the counselors, using lists of victims taken from police precinct records, knocked on doors of victims, spoke with as many as they could, and left pamphlets and flyers with them.

12. *Canvassing:* On twenty occasions, the counselors visited neighborhoods, putting flyers under all the doors.

13. *Answering Service:* A twenty-four-hour answering service in Spanish and English was installed so that crisis coverage for victims was available at all times.

14. *Health Fair:* At a health fair in the Bronx, the staff of the

THE INVISIBLE VICTIM

Crime Victims Service Center for three days maintained a workshop and booth describing the CVSC.

Direct efforts (mail, telephone, and personal contact) by the counselors resulted in the recruitment of 78 victims, about three-fourths (74 percent) of the first nine months' caseload. Included are Fordham Hospital Trauma Ward visits, where the counselors appeared regularly seeking victims of violent crime. During the first nine months the service was in operation, contact via the media was unproductive.

Telephone contact was more successful than mail recruitment. The letter is an impersonal vehicle, whereas the telephone permits the individual persuasiveness of each counselor to break down barriers of communication and trust. Also, it is possible that some victims were functional nonreaders and hence discarded the letters when received. Whatever the reasons, the rate of successful contact during the first nine months was somewhat higher by telephone than by mail. The difference is not enough, however, to warrant attaching any extraordinary significance to it.

During the last nine months the service was in operation, the project shifted its focus to a greater effort on preventive, protective, and advocacy services, while still providing individual referrals to social welfare services. During this period, we initiated a number of preventive and advocacy activities designed to raise the awareness of citizens and local community organizations to the problems of neighborhood safety. We provided information and resources to facilitate organizing activities for self-protection.

At the beginning of the project, rape victims were not eligible for our service because we were informed that the police already had such a program. We learned, however, that the police program did not provide rape prevention and education to victims. We decided, therefore, to initiate a rape prevention and education service.

A Service For Victims

Beginning in December 1974, our staffing pattern was changed to include both a field coordinator—Michael Handy, who was hired to select specific areas in which to set up prevention and advocacy programs—and a rape specialist, Yolanda Bako. Because of lack of time and resources, grass-roots community organizing was impossible. Our objective was to select already organized groups that had some resources, were aware of a particular crime problem, and wanted to do something about it.

Yolanda Bako concentrated on servicing the specific needs of rape victims and developing rape education and prevention programs. From March 1975 to the beginning of June, presentations were made to classes at each of six high schools, three colleges, as well as Metropolitan Hospital, Planned Parenthood, and Mosholu Library.

A group of thirty female medical students was organized and trained as rape victim advocates. They were on call in Jacobi Hospital emergency room from 5:00 P.M. to 8:00 A.M. seven nights a week. They provided support and companionship during the patient's stay in the emergency room, did follow-up work, and gave information on pregnancy and venereal disease prevention. They helped with preserving evidence, bathing the victim after the examination, and providing a safe place for the victim to stay during the night if she did not have one.

From the very beginning of the project, we were aware of the necessity for an information system that would record the data necessary to document our planning efforts. An excellent computerized reporting system designed by David Friedman provided us with important data concerning our service to crime victims—the first victim data generated from an actual service to victims rather than from survey interviews.

The number of self-referrals and the number of referrals made by other community agencies are two criteria indicating a service is accepted and recognized by the community. Self-referrals are the mark of a successful service and signify it has achieved visibility and legitimated itself with its prospective clients. They quadrupled during the second half of the project, becoming our most frequent source of contact.

Social service and community agency referrals as well as police and court referrals nearly doubled during the second nine months, as the program became known and utilized by community agencies.

After about a year the program had effectively established itself in the Bronx community. The increase in visibility and legitimation by victims is evidenced by the increase in "information" calls to the Crime Victims Service Center. During the first nine months we received 160 calls, mainly from the Bronx. In the second nine months 600 calls from all over the city were received.

The Victims

Who were the victims whom we assisted? What were they like? Remember, the project deliberately set about to find and help the most needy victims of crime. We reasoned that most victims of crimes of property without violence were either insured or had sufficient resources to take care of themselves.

Although we offered help to any adult resident of the Bronx who was a victim of a violent crime, our outreach efforts were directed primarily to the high-crime areas—the ghetto areas of the South Bronx.

Most young Americans have never seen a poverty area in person. They have no idea what life is like on these ravaged streets. The poor who live in this area are often described as "multiproblem" families, by welfare workers, social workers, psychologists, and psychiatrists; no single service or agency has all the facilities needed to help them. Consequently they are forced to spend inumerable hours on lines at different agencies to get help with different needs. Even though the husband is employed his earnings may be below the poverty line. If his family needs medical attention his wife may spend a whole morning or afternoon in the free clinic of a city hospital waiting her turn. I have seen people sitting for three hours on wooden benches without backs in a hospital corridor waiting to get prescriptions filled. Waiting hours for your name to be called at the welfare office only to be told you may have an appointment for two weeks later is a common experience. The needy poor of big metropolitan cities spend one-quarter to one-half of their lives on waiting lines for the basic services they need.

The bureaucratic indifference, the inconsiderate way they are treated, the rudeness they have to put up with, and the frustration of Catch-22 rules pile up until they feel nothing but cynicism, hoplessness, and frustration about social service agencies. The radio, TV, and bus ads informing them of the Crime Victims Service Center and the help available for victims of violent crime were greeted with the same cynicism. Only the most desperate made the effort until word got around the community that we really meant what we said. There were no long waiting lines. People were seen on time for their appointments and in many cases help was given.

Race and Ethnicity

The 259 victims we assisted during the eighteen months of operation were representative of the ethnic and racial populations of the Bronx. Thirty-seven percent were Black, 32 percent Hispanic, and 30 percent White.

During the first nine months more Black victims were aided than any other ethnic group. Black victims represented 42 percent of the 103 cases for this period. During the last nine months more Whites received our services. White victims represented 35 percent of the 156 cases for the period. The percentage of Hispanic victims remained approximately 30 percent for both periods. During the second period a much greater proportion of self-referrals heard about the project through the media. These were primarily White working-class or low middle-class people, and may indicate that working-class and lower middle-class Whites tended to respond to the media more frequently.

Age

The most frequent age bracket given aid was the twenty-six to forty group (33.2 percent). However, there is only a very small difference between this group and the forty-one to sixty group. Together (ages twenty-six to sixty) they constitute 64 percent of the 259 victims assisted. In general the number of cases in each age group tended to increase with the rise in age up to sixty.

It would be a mistake, however, to make any inferences about the relationship between incidence of crime and age from these figures.

Victims of murder and felonious assault tended to be in the twenty-six to forty age group. Four of the five rape victims were in the sixteen to twenty-one age group; the fifth was under sixteen.

Of the total number of clients over sixty (thirty-seven clients in all), Whites accounted for 74 percent, Blacks 11 percent, and Hispanics 14 percent. Several hypotheses could explain the high concentration of White elderly victims in the group utilizing the services of our center. One reason may be that many of the elderly Whites whom we serviced lived in neighborhoods where the racial balance had shifted, and crime rates were higher. Living within the bounds of a fixed income does not offer many opportunities for moving away from a neighborhood. In New York City many of the elderly reside in rent-controlled apartments and cannot move because they would be subject to new rent laws by which their rents would drastically increase. Many elderly Whites choose to remain in neighborhoods where they have lived for years, although the areas have deteriorated and are crime-ridden. Fear of the unknown is greater than familiar fear. Many people are unwilling to leave homes in which they raised families. Memories are sometimes impossible to leave.

Mrs. Englemann's three-room, $100-a-month apartment is filled with the memories of a lifetime—fading photographs of her two children, the piano they played on when they were growing up, their old clothes. Has she ever thought about moving to a safer neighborhood? "I'm not moving, let them go to hell!" she shouted. "I'm stubborn. Why should I give up the apartment I've lived in for 32 years? My children grew up here. We were all happy. We had parties. Even my younger sister got married here. Why don't they just keep those monsters in jail where they belong?"[1]

Another explanation of the high level of White elderly victims is that their physical and social isolation may be greater than that of Black and Hispanic people. In the South Bronx, at least, many Black and Hispanic elderly are part of extended families. They often live with their families and help working mothers raise the children.

Finally, a third factor that may explain the higher proportion of White elderly victims is racial hostility. This is especially evident in violent attacks on elderly White victims by youths who make racial comments. Many of these attacks involve outrageous physical brutality, where profit is not the motive and the elderly victim is unable to offer resistance.

For all these reasons, it appears to me that elderly Whites are victimized far more than other White victims. A program to help elderly crime victims would probably provide services to a high proportion of Whites.

Sex

Although more male victims (56 percent) were serviced than female victims (44 percent), the difference was not significant. However, where a homicide was involved the client was female in 71 percent of the cases—probably because the client was the wife or mother of the victim.

Two-thirds of the 181 victims of felonious assault were males. The fact that one-third of the victims were female gave us a higher percentage than we anticipated. Women who are victims of felonious assaults perpetrated by ex-boyfriends or ex-husbands live in terror of the offender or his cohorts, fearing injury to themselves or their children if they prosecute the case. No protective services are available to them.

White victims tended to be female (and elderly). Black and Hispanic victims tended to be male.

Crime Category

Aggravated assault was the most frequent crime suffered by the victims we serviced. Victims of homicide and aggravated assault constituted 78 percent of the 259 who came for help. Assault was the major criminal offense in both high- and low-crime areas. The highest proportion of assault victims (48 percent) were in the twenty-six to sixty age group. Under twenty-six years old accounted for 20 percent of the victims. Ten percent were over sixty.

All ethnic and racial groups suffered equally from aggravated assaults. The distribution was:

Black	74 percent
Hispanic	77 percent
White	61 percent

The average middle-class citizen has the impression that robbery is the most frequent violent crime. But statistics for the entire nation show aggravated assaults to be slightly more frequent than robberies. In our cases, however, assaults were six times more frequent than robberies.

When people express concern about "crime in the streets," they are generally referring to mugging, rape, and other crimes in which they imagine being attacked by a stranger. The media, the police, and politicians constantly reinforce this image as evidence of a breakdown of law and order. These crimes are, of course, frequent enough to cause concern. But if aggravated assault is the most frequent violent crime, then the major problem is not the chance of being "accidentally" assaulted on the streets by a stranger. By far the greatest number of aggravated assaults and homicides involve members of the same family or acquaintances from the same neighborhood or work group. Violent crime is more frequently closely associated with a breakdown in interpersonal relationships than a breakdown of law and order. As far as violent crime is concerned, "crime in the house"—in the symbolic sense—seems to be a deeper and more widespread problem than "crime in the streets." Work with the family may be a key to a more profound approach to the problem of crime than the usual demogogic denunciation of crime in the streets.

Victim Needs

To determine the needs of victims, we recorded what they indicated was the most important problem with which they wanted help.

Most Important Problem Indicated by Victim

Class of Problem	# of Victims	Percentage
Financial assistance	124	47.9
Legal	29	11.2
Physical health	29	11.2
Emotional health	24	9.3
Housing	21	8.1
Employment	13	6.9
Household management	6	2.3
No most important problem	7	2.7
Total	259	

Close to half the victims indicated that *immediate* financial assistance was their most important problem. Legal services and services for physical and emotional health were next in order of frequency.

We felt the necessity to record more specifically the exact nature of the need even though it may not have been considered as the most important by the client. For example although 171 clients listed specific financial needs only 124 listed financial assistance as their most important need.

Specific Financial Assistance Needs Indicated by Victim

Specific Need	# of Victims	Percentage
Reimbursement for loss and living expenses	98	57.2
Medical care expenses	42	24.6
Family care	15	8.8
Housing	2	1.2
Legal and business expenses	2	1.2
Other	12	7.0
Total	171	

Victims who indicated that financial assistance was their most important problem also needed financial help for medical care, family care, and for immediate food and living expenses. These three needs make up 91 percent of the reasons for the need for emergency financial aid.

These tables were not created out of mere verbal responses to a questionnaire. They are based on the urgent and sometimes desperate calls for help from people who had been physically harmed and suffered severe financial loss (in an already deprived situation, with 43 percent on income maintenance or Social Security) with no resources to back them up. Neither the frequency tables nor the term "financial assistance" conveys the *urgency* and *immediacy* of the need. "Emergency financial aid" or even "disaster aid" more closely describes the condition.

THE INVISIBLE VICTIM

Specific Physical Health Needs Indicated by Victim

Service Need	# of Victims	Percentage
Hospital care or clinic	37	46.2
Physical impairment	13	16.2
Doctor's care	8	10.0
Medical costs	8	10.0
Continued care	5	6.3
Dental	3	3.8
Other	6	7.5
Total	80	

Forty-six percent who had crime-related physical health needs required hospital or clinic care. Sixteen percent had permanent impairment caused by the crime.

Specific Emotional Health Needs Indicated by Victim

Specific Need	# of Victims	Percentage
Hospital care or clinic	18	40.0
Client in shock (no medical attention)	12	26.7
Continued care	6	13.3
Doctor's care	1	2.2
Medical costs	1	2.2
Other	7	15.5
Total	45	

Twenty-seven percent had severe emotional problems, were in a state of confusion and helplessness, and had received no medical attention. Forty percent of those with emotional trauma required hospital or clinic care.

Specific Employment Needs Indicated by Victim

Specific Need	# of Victims	Percentage
Placement	28	57.1
Training or retraining	10	20.4
Lost time	5	10.2
Cannot work (Workman's Compensation)	4	8.2
More income	1	2.0
Other	1	2.0
Total	49	

Job placement was requested by 57 percent. They had either lost their job or were unable to work at their old job as a result of the crime. Twenty percent needed training or retraining in order to work.

Specific Legal Needs Indicated by Victim

Specific Need	# of Victims	Percentage
Lawyer for legal service or advice	14	31.1
Court appearance	14	31.1
Protection	12	26.6
D. A.'s assistance insufficient	3	6.6
Present lawyer unsatisfactory	1	2.2
Other	1	2.2
Total	45	

Thirty-one percent of the victims required a lawyer for legal action or advice. Help with court appearances (victim-witnesses) was requested by 31 percent. Twenty-seven percent wanted legal help for protection (safety).

Specific Housing Needs Indicated by Victim

Specific Need	# of Victims	Percentage
Move—emotional trauma	16	33.3
Safety	13	27.1
Larger number of rooms	7	14.6
Housing costs	2	4.1
Other	10	20.8
Total	48	

Physical harm causes high levels of fear of continued victimization and generates a desire to relocate in what is believed to be a safer area. Thirty-three percent of the victims wanted to move because of emotional trauma associated with their present living arrangement.

Summary of Needs

By far, the most frequent need expressed by victims was for immediate financial aid (48 percent). The second most frequent need was for physical health care (11 percent). If we combine the number of requests for physical health care with those for emotional health care, the percentage increases to 21 percent. The third ranked need was for legal assistance (11 percent). At least 31 percent of those who needed legal assistance were victim-witnesses.

Significantly, when victims were asked what was the second most important problem for which they needed help, 45 percent did *not* express a problem. Almost half of the victims came for one reason only. They had one serious need, and they sought assistance for that alone.

Considering the fact that we were dealing with what is referred to as a "multi-problem population," some of whom were very "social-agency–wise" and could under ordinary circumstances negotiate their way through the bureaucratic maze of social agencies, this was additional evidence of the traumatic effect of victimization and the urgency of need. Victims tended to have one desperate need; their other needs could wait.

It is important to keep in mind that the frequencies of these needs were given by a particular population of victims. It would be unwarranted to assume that all victims of violent crime would express the same hierarchy of needs. Certainly victims from a population of higher socioeconomic status would have economic and financial resources that might change the frequency with which immediate financial aid and medical assistance were needed. Moreover, some of the victims we saw may have come to the center expecting to be given financial aid—that is, in the hope of finding a service more responsive than other services to their general economic situation. In fact, many of them refused our service when they discovered we were not able to provide direct financial assistance. On the other hand, even those who were better off financially often found themselves reduced to indigency by medical or funeral costs as well as by unemployment or lost days at work.

Although we cannot say that the frequencies of needs expressed by our population truly represent the hierarchy of needs of all victims, we can with certainty maintain that the population of victims we saw was a representative sample of the majority of victims of violent crime in the inner city and that they expected a service to provide them with aid in the order cited.

While I must be careful about the generalizability of the project's findings, I do not want to take the blood out of the experience by citing all the qualifying circumstances which give the appearance of a vigorous scientific approach. The victims we saw were representative of the majority of victims of violent crime in the "inner city." They genuinely needed money, a doctor, and a lawyer, and they needed it immediately.

Services Provided

Documentation of the services provided produced important data about the responsiveness of existing agencies to the needs of victims; the availability of services for specific needs; the utilization patterns of victims; and the degree of success that can be expected from a victim assistance program that depends largely on referrals to other service organizations.

A total of 217 referrals were made—108 to the Crime Victims Compensation Board of New York State (CVCB) and 109 to other human service agencies. The remaining 42 needed translation assistance only, or help with filling out forms, or no services existed for them. Because the Crime Victims Compensation Board is the only agency that is specifically designated for victims of crime, results of referrals to the CVCB will be discussed separately from the results of the other service agencies.

SUMMARY OF THE RESULTS OF REFERRALS TO SERVICE AGENCIES

In the following summary you will notice that a relatively high number of victims declined to follow through with our referrals to the various agencies. The reasons for it and the implications for the design of future services for victims will be discussed later in this chapter.

1. Forty-one of the 259 victims were referred to the Welfare Department for financial assistance and housing. Slightly more than half (23) were accepted, not for emergency aid but for routine processing. Three were refused service by the agency and fourteen declined our referral.
2. Ten victims were referred to the Social Security Agency. Four were accepted, three placed on the waiting list, one was rejected, and two declined our referral.
3. Eleven victims were referred for Medicaid or Medicare. Eight were accepted, two placed on waiting lists, one declined service.

A Service For Victims

4. Seven victims were referred to the Vocational Rehabilitation Agency. Three were accepted, four declined the referral.

5. Eighteen victims were referred to Community Service Corporations for mental health services, job training, or emergency financial aid. Three were accepted, two were refused service by the agency, three were placed on a waiting list, and ten declined our referral.

6. Sixteen victims were referred to the Court Appearance Control Project. Ten were accepted, one placed on the waiting list, and five declined our referral. (This project developed a computerized system to notify victim witnesses of the date and time they were to appear in court. It was designed to eliminate the necessity of people sitting in court all day waiting to be heard.)

7. Six victims were referred for Workman's Compensation. Only one victim was accepted, four were refused service. One declined the referral.

8. More than half (138) of the victims received individual counseling, which is not to be confused with therapy. The counseling consisted primarily of advising victims how to cope with the situation, explaining resources available, providing an opportunity for ventilation, and giving friendly support.

9. More than a third (91) of the victims needed assistance with filling out forms. In some cases victims were so discouraged by the bureaucratic red tape that, rather than fill out the forms, they refused to follow through on the referral.

10. Only twenty victims required personal representation at the agency referred to. We were puzzled by this finding, since we felt that one of the major functions of the nonprofessional counselor was to represent the victim. However, it appears that our liaison arrangements were frequently effective enough to enable the counselor to use the phone to represent the victim.

11. Escort services to victims (18) were reduced by the existence of the Court Appearance Control Project and by the reluctance of frightened victims to venture out even with an escort. Also, some victims such as the aged needed escort services on a continuing basis, a service this project could not deliver.

12. Forty-nine victims needed translation assistance. This is further evidence of the need for bilingual staff in agencies dealing with victims.

Service Gaps

Finding emergency financial aid for victims was virtually impossible. Thirty-four out of the 124 who needed financial aid eventually received help, but not on an emergency basis. Only one victim received funds within twenty-four hours; funds for the remainder took anywhere from two weeks to five months.

Ten victims who needed court appearance services were accommodated. No other legal services could be found for nineteen victims who needed a lawyer. Eighteen victims were intimidated or threatened with violence if they pressed charges or testified. Six elderly persons were harassed or threatened with revictimization. Eleven, not elderly (under sixty), were also intimidated by threats of violence. No protection services could be found for these thirty-five victims.

New York State Crime Victims Compensation Board Referrals

The Crime Victims Compensation Board is the only public agency specifically designated to serve victims of crime. Its record with respect to victims is worse than any other public agency. The average length of time for an award to be made is from five to nine months. Our counselors were trained by the CVCB personnel to fill out forms and prescreen applicants. In very few cases did this shorten the period of waiting. Applicants to the CVCB are often in an emergency financial situation, needing funeral funds and other such assistance. By the time an award is made the applicant may be in debt and have to pay interest and loan costs. The application procedure was cumbersome to a ridiculous degree—for example, it required a signed affidavit from a funeral parlor that the victim had been buried. Innumerable forms had to be filled out and notorized, receipts for expenditures produced, and so on.

More than a third of the victims (108) were referred to the CVCB. During the entire life of the project, only eleven of them were accepted as eligible, processing completed, and an award made within five months. Five were declared ineligible. Eleven declined the referral. The eligibility of eighty-one was still pending when the project closed.

The CVCB waits to see if financial assistance is given by other sources such as Workman's Compensation or Blue Cross-Blue Shield. It did not have a bilingual staff member to assist Hispanic applicants. And the CVCB makes little effort to provide the public with information regarding its services. We could not accept their explanation that there was no money in the budget for such activities, since free public service announcements are certainly available.

In the final report[2] of the Crime Victims Service Center, we made the following recommendations for improving the services of the CVCB.

1. The application procedure should be simplified and streamlined.
2. The CVCB be authorized to make emergency awards within forty-eight hours.
3. The custom of waiting to see if the victim is reimbursed by other agencies be abandoned. The CVCB could make awards based on the fact of victimization. A procedure could be instituted similar to that used in Good Samaritan awards, in which a lien may be placed against awards made later on by other agencies and the amount of the CVCB's award deducted.
4. The CVCB should train personnel in other social agencies to pre-screen applicants.
5. A bilingual staff member should be employed. (Twenty-two percent of the CVSC total caseload were Spanish speaking only.)
6. A widespread public information program should be instituted, making use of the media to inform the public of the services of the CVCB.

THE INVISIBLE VICTIM

We engaged in some advocacy efforts to make the New York State Crime Victims Compensation Board more responsive. During community presentations we raised issues relating to the narrow guidelines for example, the means test, and slow pace of that agency; we urged people to contact elected officials to voice their outrage regarding this program; on a legislative level, we worked with a member of the New York State Senate who had drawn up new legislation proposing significant changes in the operation of the New York State Crime Victims Compensation Board. We also met with representatives of the New York State Legislative Commission on Expenditure Review who were conducting an audit of Crime Victims Compensation Board activities. We were assured that our recommendations concerning changes in the existing legislation would receive careful attention.

NEWS ITEM [3]

The most recent report of the New York State Crime Victims Compensation Board, summarizing its work from April 1, 1974, to March 30, 1975, states that it received 2,341 claims during this period. An average of 40 percent of the applications on file received compensation. The proportion of awards as against the number of people injured or killed is miniscule because of provisions in the crime victims compensation law and the circumstances surrounding the application. The legislators seemed convinced that a large number of victims stood to profit handsomely if compensated for their hurts, and therefore restricted eligibility to certain kinds of losses, by a form of means test, and by making the compensation the last resource.

The law does provide for payment to an innocent victim for any out-of-pocket unreimbursed medical expenses and actual unrecovered loss of earnings for a period of more than two weeks. In the event of death, compensation is available to a widow or dependent children.

A primary obstacle to acceptance of a claim is that the victim must prove "serious financial hardship." At the discretion of the Crime Victims Compensation Board savings equal to a year's earnings can be exempted. Still, the means test, with its attendant demands for documentation, discourages applicants where it does not actually disqualify them.

A Service For Victims

... Until now, the burden of supplying proof of financial hardship, out-of-pocket costs and even the fact that a crime of violence was visited upon them lay entirely on the victim. "Just going into a police station to get a police report number could be very difficult for some people," says Chairman Edward A. Morrison of the Crime Compensation Board. The absence of bilingual forms deterred many Spanish-speaking residents from filing. A new system now mandates that one of the twelve investigators sees every claimant. Together, they will collect the necessary papers for review by a member of the board.

There remain, however, many inequities in the law. Pat Henson says, "If a wage earner loses an arm or leg the only compensation will be for the medical bills and for wages lost while he was actually hospitalized. Unlike most insurance policies, there is no provision for the loss of earnings because the victim can no longer perform his former job."

The law bars payments to victims who are related or have an "affinity" to the third consanguinity. That extends through children, siblings, uncles, aunts, nephews, and nieces. If an uncle shoots the parents of children, the orphans do not qualify. Anyone with an ongoing "sexual relationship" is ineligible if victimized by the partner.

The invisibility of New York's program reflects a lack of publicity about its existence. "We have no budget for publicity," explains Mr. Petromelis. However, 70,000 brochures have been distributed to community agencies and a series of letters has been addressed to hospital officials. Because victims' compensation provides payments where none might be forthcoming, doctors and hospital administrators encourage patients to fill out the papers. But if society is serious about making amends to those it has failed to protect, then it would seem obligated to advise its citizens of the compensation program.

I am pleased to report that the 1977 annual report of the New York State Crime Victims Compensation Board[4] indicates that a number of changes have been made along the lines we suggested. These changes have made the New York State CVCB one of the better victim compensation programs of the twenty states that have passed such legislation. A complete discussion of the issues and problems as well as a model crime victims' compensation law will be presented in chapter 6.

What We Learned about Servicing Victims of Violent Crime

THE ISSUE OF VICTIMS' NEEDS

The professional social welfare worker has a two-part definition of victims' needs. On one level, victims' needs are defined from the point of view of professional values of fair and just entitlements of the people who are victimized. On the practical level, victims' needs are often defined by the institutional practices of the particular agency in which the professional works.

The professional view of needs differs from the "felt need" of victims. The victims' view of their needs is also perceived in several different ways. The *retrospective* view is held by people who have been victimized in the past; it expresses what they can recall they needed at the time they were victimized. This differs from the *reactive* view, in which people who are in a state of crisis because of victimization express their immediate needs. This difference is evident in the discrepancy between survey statistics and the data from our service delivery. In the survey the most frequently expressed need was police services. The second was medical assistance, and the third was financial assistance. This ranking does not correspond to the frequency of the needs expressed by the victims who were actually using our service; as noted, for them the most important services needed were emergency financial assistance, medical assistance, and legal assistance, in that order.

In addition, there is another level of needs, which consists of a variety of feelings and emotions regarding social justice. The victims want the criminal punished and removed from the streets so as not to bother them again, and they want to feel that they don't have to be afraid of asking for justice.

64

A Service For Victims

Need must be distinguished from *demand* or *utilization.* What people *say* they need is not necessarily any indication of how much effort they are willing to make to satisfy that need. It would be a mistake to assume, on the other hand, that the lack of utilization of services is an indication of lack of "felt need." More than likely apathy, hopelessness, and frustration are learned reactions to previous attempts to utilize services.

As noted, the reasons a victims' service such as the one we offered was not maximally utilized include:

1. Securing the names of victims from the police put us in the position of being considered an arm of the police. Victims who are suspicious and distrustful of the police reacted to us in the same manner.
2. Some victims of violent crime are "marginal" victims, that is, they have been or in some cases are as much offenders as they are victims, and expect to be treated as offenders rather than as victims. They therefore shy away from any contact with the police or with any agency that appears to be tied to the police. This is especially true in felonious assault cases.
3. Many of the victims regard service agencies with suspicion and distrust fostered by repeated experiences of bureaucratic indifference.
4. Many victims are terrorized, fear reprisal, and do not wish to make themselves visible.
5. There is a general tendency among the poor in high-crime areas to react with resignation and acceptance of victimization as a condition of life.
6. Among certain ethnic groups people in need turn to their own families and friends rather than turning to public service agencies.

THE ISSUE OF DIRECT OR REFERRAL SERVICE

When victims discovered we offered no direct services ourselves but only referrals to other agencies, they often reacted with disappointment and a feeling of having been "conned" again. They required much urging to follow through. Some never did. This undoubtedly accounts for the large number of victims who declined or refused our referrals (22 percent of those referred).

The reluctant utilizer of services who has an emergency is sensitive to any delay in getting help. A delay simply reinforces their hesitant attitude. Delays caused by excessive forms to fill out, waiting periods, appointment schedules, referrals to other agencies, and so on, tend to discourage victims even when their situation is desperate.

Also, the service agencies are not geared toward handling emergencies. In one sense, all of their cases are emergencies and therefore are handled in a routine manner. The only real emergencies they recognize are those of a natural disaster. The complete pauperization of a victim is not considered an emergency, let alone a disaster.

I seriously question the feasibility of a service for victims that offers no direct assistance but is primarily a referral service acting as a bridge between the criminal justice system and the human service system.

THE ISSUE OF COUNSELOR MORALE

The program relied on trained paraprofessionals to deliver its referral services. They were intelligent, indigenous people, some of whom still lived in the area they worked. Unquestionably, they were representative of our victim population. The advantages of employing this type of staff were: (1) familiarity with the community—they knew the right organizations and community leaders to contact; (2) communication with the victims was facilitated; (3) outreach efforts were more easily affected.

However, we found that despite high enthusiasm at the beginning, within a few months the counselors absorbed and reflected the hopeless, frustrated, and apathetic attitudes of the victims. Intensive efforts to modify these feelings failed. Because of this experience we hesitated to propose a city-wide referral agency staffed by thirty to forty indigenous paraprofessionals.

Discussion of Results

To help victims with *immediate emergency financial aid, medical care,* and *legal services,* would take the combined efforts of the social welfare system, the human service system and the criminal justice system, including the courts and police.

Our experience demonstrated that emergency financial aid is not available. The social welfare system is not responsive to the "emergency" nature of the situation, not because there are no funds available but because of the institutional policies, rules, and regulations of the agencies involved, which do not define victimization as a "disaster" warranting emergency procedures. *The need therefore is not to expedite processing but rather to change system policies to make such disaster aid possible.*

Medical care is available, although at times it is slow and inadequate. Trained expediters can help victims negotiate their way through the medical bureaucratic labyrinth. Medical personnel in emergency rooms need to be trained in procedures to assist rape victims to collect and preserve evidence, give them support and encouragement to report the crime, and deal with the specific emotional trauma associated with it.

The need for legal services is primarily a matter of responsiveness, requiring expediting services to assist the individual victim as well as system changes in the institutional policies and practices of the courts and the legal profession.

Lawyers and the courts more often than not ignore the victim. Judges postpone trials without the slightest consideration of the victim's situation or needs.

Police have developed little or no procedure for dealing with victims and their needs. As high as 20 percent of names and addresses given by victims to the police are false or obsolete. That the police have not developed procedures for securing more reliable information, at least about where to find the victim, seems unbelievable. If the police are dealing with such a transient victim population that 20 percent no longer can be found at the addresses given two to five weeks after the crime, then they ought to develop more effective information procedures, such as identifying next of kin or asking for a second permanent address at which the victim can be reached. However, I do not mean to imply that 20 percent of victims are transient. There are many other reasons why victims give the police false names and addresses. The program staff was convinced that the victim-offender described earlier constituted the bulk of those victims giving the police false names and addresses.

The police are under great pressure to apprehend offenders. They have little time, knowledge, or incentive for dealing with victims. Protection for threatened victims is unavailable.

Special Status

We identified the target population as those victims of violent crime from low economic groups, the elderly poor, and victims of rape. Are these victims entitled to at least the same consideration as the offenders who have been granted "special status" that entitles them to heavy investments in public funds for remedial purposes?

Victims are often considered in the same demeaning manner as are people on welfare. Social welfare agencies do not grant victims special status, and no distinction is made between *victims* who need social welfare services and other clients. Except for the CVCB, victims are not considered entitled to any special consideration. And the CVCB, the one agency that does grant victims special status, is the least effective public agency when it comes to servicing victims.

A Service For Victims

Those who are totally without resources as a result of a crime constitute a human disaster class of victims that needs special services and should be granted special status by the human service and criminal justice systems.

To sum up, we concluded that a large proportion of services to victims would require major system changes, as well as major efforts to develop expediting services for individual victims. Addressing the needs of the individual victim attacks the problem episodically; each case becomes a crisis. Systematically identifying problems of victims and addressing the appropriate system changes needed can help individual victims more effectively. At the same time, the needs of individual victims on a day-to-day basis cannot be ignored. The first task, system change, requires advocacy on behalf of all victims, while the second requires expediting efforts on behalf of individual victims.

Changing the criminal justice and social welfare systems to make them more responsive to the needs of all victims requires an advocacy model which is totally different from a victim-assistance model designed to expedite service to individual victims. Effective service to individual victims should come from within the system. The system must become responsive enough to dispense with the need for a middleman expediter.

At the present time there are several models of service to victims. Most, like ours, are federally funded through LEAA. They break down into those that only service victim-witnesses participating in court processes and those that service a more diverse victim population, attempting to bridge the gap between the social service and criminal justice systems.

THE VICTIM-WITNESS MODEL

The rationale for this model is to increase the number of victim-witnesses who press charges and follow through in prosecuting offenders. The advantage of these programs is the ease of identifying the target population, which thus eliminates the need for time-consuming, costly outreach efforts. Specific needs of victims can also be pinpointed with relative ease—for example, transportation to and from court, day care, and access to a convenient room in which to await testimony. This concept offers quick results and measurable achievement in addressing the individual needs of victim-witnesses.

The Court Appearance Control Project is an example of effective service rendered by this model to individual victims. However, significant gaps exist in this model. Few programs address themselves to the system changes necessary to aid victim-witnesses as a group. Little is done about the criminal justice system's failure to convey a sense of justice to victims. More concretely, little attention is paid to the problem of restitution, and mechanisms directed at protection and safety of the victim-witnesses are rare.

The most serious limitation of this model is its concentration on the small number of victims that reach the court. Hence, only a small proportion of victims receive any services whatsoever.

THE REFERRAL SERVICE MODEL

The advantage of the referral model, of which the Crime Victims Service Center was an example, is that it services victims outside the court system. This model is conceived of as a bridge between the criminal justice system and the social welfare system. The difficulties, however, are many; locating victims and the absence of timely and effective services for their needs are only two of the problems. Servicing a broader target population makes it difficult to concentrate available resources on manageable problems. Given the fact that many victims are from low-income areas, the social service referral approach is further complicated by the high incidence of multi-problem people whose service needs brought on by victimization represent only a fraction of their total needs.

Any service offered in a victim program must do more than provide information on where to secure help. In a city such as New York, a "road map" of available services is of little use.

A Service For Victims

The victim is often unable to find the way through the jungle of social service programs and agencies.

One of the more serious problems with this model is the fragmentation of the social welfare services. Each service has its own rules and regulations, its eligibility requirements, and so on. It often happens that one agency may refuse service because of its eligibility requirements and refer the client to another agency. The other agency also refuses service because of some technicality. The victim thus "falls between the cracks" of the fragmented services.

Another difficulty with this model is that victims become discouraged when immediate direct service is not available.

Under these circumstances to speak of building a bridge between the criminal justice system and the social welfare system is like proposing to build a bridge on pylons sunk in quicksand.

THE CENTRALIZED DIRECT SERVICE MODEL

A third option would be a model in which a new agency, independent of the criminal justice and social welfare systems, would be created. It would provide all the services needed by victims. This model is not very feasible because: (1) it adds another agency and bureaucracy to a social service system already too fragmented; (2) manpower and other resources would take years to acquire; and (3) it would be too costly.

THE DECENTRALIZED DIRECT SERVICE MODEL

This model requires no new agency or bureaucratic apparatus. The staffs of the criminal justice and social welfare agencies could be trained as victim counselors. The disadvantage of this model is that institutional policies of these agencies make it impossible to service the special needs of victims. To be viable, this model requires recognition of the special status of victims and substantial changes in policy, rules, and regulations.

THE ADVOCACY MODEL

The advocacy model would create an organization to act as spokesman for victims. It would focus on the problems of victims in general as well as assist individual victims. Rather than look at one case at a time, it would place its emphasis on the necessary changes in the criminal justice and social welfare systems. A program organized under the advocacy model would look at the whole problem of aid to victims, including preventive, protective, legal, and social services. It would conduct investigations, promote legislative action, and organize public support for system changes necessary to increase the range of services available to victims.

Conclusion

After studying the needs of violent-crime victims and the response of the criminal justice and human service systems to these needs for two years, the Crime Victims Service Center made the following recommendation to the Mayor's Criminal Justice Coordinating Council of New York City.[5]

Considering all the data, observations, issues, and options, we concluded that the most effective service for victims of violent crime in New York City would be a private nonprofit or quasi-public victims' advocacy center that would combine the characteristics of an advocacy model with those of a decentralized direct service model.

Such a center's major focus would be to serve as spokesman for victims for:

1. Changes in the social welfare agencies to make them more responsive to the emergency needs of victims.
2. Changes in the criminal justice system to make it more responsive to the legal, restitutive, and protection needs of victims.
3. The legislative action necessary to assist victims. It would also attempt to inform the public and organize support to bring about

the necessary legislative or system changes in the interest of victims.

Such a center would implement these activities by conducting training programs for existing personnel in the social welfare and criminal justice systems designated as victim counselors. It would also provide such training to designated personnel in private or semi-private organizations such as the Bar Association, community organizations, and private medical facilities.

It would also act as an information center, operating a "hot line" to inform victims about social, legal, and other services available. And finally, it would provide consultation on preventive programs to community groups, tenants' associations, senior citizens' clubs, etc.

Such an agency or organization, in our opinion, combines the best features of the various models while avoiding most of the difficulties associated with them.

Locating the service outside of the public sector would enable it to lobby and use litigation efforts to a greater degree than a public agency could.

This recommendation was followed by a detailed plan and budget for the operation of a Crime Victims Advocacy Center. Some of these proposals will be discussed in later chapters.

The report concluded with these words:

We believe that a Victims Advocacy Center is the most feasible and best way to serve the victims of violent crime in New York City at this time. Given the present contraction of services and economic crisis it is also the most economical.

However, we believe that under different social and economic conditions we would not propose anything different. Our experience with the Crime Victims Service Center has convinced us that the major approach has to be toward system changes in the Criminal Justice and the Social Welfare systems and that direct services should be anchored in the services themselves based on such changes.

We would like to say that though we have been critical of both the Criminal Justice and Social Welfare systems, no criticism of any individual in either system is implied. We have found many people in both systems sympathetic to the needs of victims and willing to help. But, for the most part, the system made it difficult or impossible. It is not the individuals that make the system ineffective but the system that makes those within it unable to help victims.[6]

THE INVISIBLE VICTIM

This report was submitted on September 30, 1975, to the Honorable Benjamin Altman, Chairman of the Criminal Justice Coordinating Council (CJCC), Office of the Mayor of New York City. At this writing—April 1978—I have received no official word from them about the report. The only evidence I have that they read it is a news item about the report by William Clairborne of the *Washington Post* dated January 4, 1976. To my knowledge, the following excerpt from that news item is all that has ever been said formally and publicly about that report. " 'The financial situation doesn't really leave much room for these recommendations. I don't know what we can do with them,' said Ziporah Twersky, the project's planning coordinator [Actually, she was the monitor of the CVSC for the CJCC.] and a member of the city's Criminal Justice Coordinating Council."[7]

One final note. I believe it was in May 1976 I visited the offices of the Law Enforcement Assistance Administration in Washington—the agency that had supplied $330,000 of public money for the Crime Victims Service Center—to find out if they intended to send the information we had gathered to other victim assistance programs, or if they were using the information in designing new programs. I spent half a day trying to find someone who had read the report. No one there even knew of its existence. Not too easily discouraged, I offered to send them a copy that they could read, duplicate, and send to investigators in the field who were conducting these programs. The young bureaucrat—I think he was a lawyer—officiously informed me that if I wanted them to read the report and disseminate the information it contained I would have to fill out an application to designate the program as an "exemplary project." He handed me an application and a brochure with some very nice, expensive-looking artwork on the cover. My thoughts were not very professional at that moment and I let him know it. I also understood how such wasteful, officious, and arrogant practices on the part of a criminal justice agency produces in the disenfranchised victim, the cynicism, wariness, and disgust they frequently exhibit toward the system.

CHAPTER 4

POST-CRIME VICTIMIZATION

The worst thing about becoming a victim is what happens after the crime. Once you become a victim you are propelled into a series of post-crime victimizations. The traumatic effects of a violent crime are multiplied by neglect, lack of immediate remedial resources, and the failure of such support systems as the courts, the police, the legal profession, and for the poor the health, welfare, and other human service agencies as well. Victims are not given the opportunity to recover from the criminal onslaught—they are repetitively dealt social and emotional blows.

The symbol of blind justice is not meant as a directive to the policeman, the district attorney, and the judge to be blind to the *person* who was wronged by the offender. But the dictum that the offender has committed a crime against the state leaves victims in criminal court without the means for redress of the wrong done to them. To victims justice means their right as an aggrieved party *to be made whole again*—immediately and with no hassle. The *victim* is entitled to justice for himself as the person wronged. I cannot say the criminal justice system is concerned with justice for the *offender*. Its primary interest is in processing the offender, and it views the victim as nothing more than a piece of evidence.

Compare the treatment given to offenders with that given to victims by the "criminal injustice system" shown in figure 1.

Public sentiment has compelled the courts to be sensitive to the rights of offenders, but responsiveness to the rights of victims—(which ought to have kept pace)—has been neglected. Victims are an oppressed minority. Today the victim, rather than the offender, is more often maltreated by the American system of justice.

Post-crime victimization is inflicted not only by the criminal justice system but the human service system as well. One might expect the system designed to assist the needy to respond quickly to the catastrophe of victimization. But the social service system does not acknowledge the "emergency" needs of victims.

The victim is treated by the human service system as a welfare supplicant, not as a person unwittingly damaged with the right to be made whole again.

Post-crime victimization is not simply a matter of bureaucratic indifference. The solution is not simply a matter of more humane treatment by the people working in the system. The more important issue is changing system policies.

This chapter will discuss in detail the various ways the police, the courts, the legal profession, and the human service system contribute to post-crime victimization.

The Police

In most cases, the police are not actually witnesses to a crime. They respond to a call after a crime has been committed. In common police practice arrests for misdemeanors are made only when the police witness the crime or when a warrant has been issued. To obtain a warrant the victim must appear before the police or the district attorney and make a written complaint. If there is sufficient reason to believe that a felony has been committed and that the person identified as the offender committed the crime, the police can make an arrest on "probable cause" or "reasonable belief." These highly subjective criteria provide the police with much discretionary power.

Low arrest rates (52 percent for rape, 64 percent for aggravated assault, and only 27 percent for robbery)[1]* can be attributed to: (1) failure to apprehend the offender; (2) the exercise by police of discretionary power not to make an arrest because of insufficient evidence; or (3) the reluctance of the victim to press charges or be a witness. Most people think the low arrest rate is caused by the failure of the police to apprehend an offender or the reluctance of the victim to provide information. But in the largest number of cases, arrests are not made because the police have exercised their discretionary power not to make one, even though, in many cases, they *know* who the offender is.

Morris and Hawkins[2] report:

The Center for the Studies in Criminal Justice at the University of Chicago ran a service called Legal Services to Youth, providing legal assistance to children and youths arrested in a ghetto area northwest of the university. It is an area with the highest or second highest delinquency crime rate in Chicago. We found that of every hundred youths arrested, only forty reached the court intake process. Of those forty, only twenty actually reached the court. Those figures are accurate; the next figure is a guess, but we think it is a reasonably informed guess. We believe, and the police in the area share this view, that the hundred that they arrested represented five hundred "probable cause" arrest situations.

So five hundred arrest situations on the streets were reduced to a hundred arrests, reduced later to forty court intakes, reduced to twenty in court, and then, of those twenty, a very few found themselves in the correctional system. Thus, the police decided more often than the judges

* These are the percentage of offenses "cleared" by arrests. See discussion in Chapter 2.

Figure 1

THE CRIMINAL INJUSTICE SYSTEM

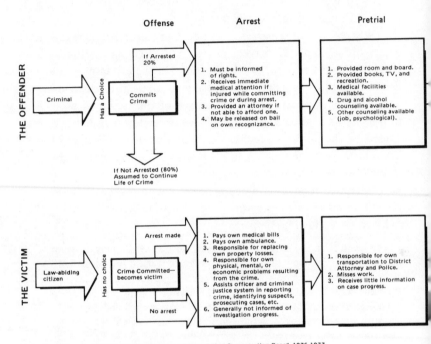

Note: Adapted by permission from the New York State Crime Victims Compensation Board, 1976-1977 Review of the Tenth Year of Operations, p. 4.

Trial	Sentencing	Sentence	Post-Release

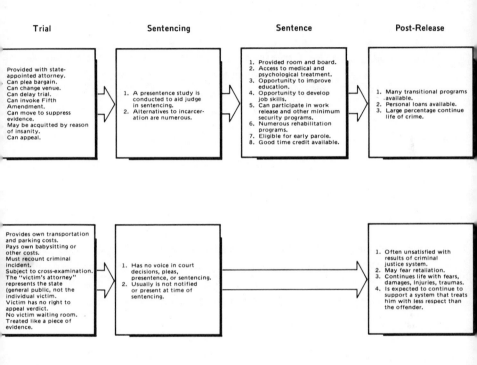

Trial

Provided with state-appointed attorney.
Can plea bargain.
Can change venue.
Can delay trial.
Can invoke Fifth Amendment.
Can move to suppress evidence.
May be acquitted by reason of insanity.
Can appeal.

Sentencing

1. A presentence study is conducted to aid judge in sentencing.
2. Alternatives to incarceration are numerous.

Sentence

1. Provided room and board.
2. Access to medical and psychological treatment.
3. Opportunity to improve education.
4. Opportunity to develop job skills.
5. Can participate in work release and other minimum security programs.
6. Numerous rehabilitation programs.
7. Eligible for early parole.
8. Good time credit available.

Post-Release

1. Many transitional programs available.
2. Personal loans available.
3. Large percentage continue life of crime.

Provides own transportation and parking costs.
Pays own babysitting or other costs.
Must recount criminal incident.
Subject to cross-examination.
The "victim's attorney" represents the state (general public, not the individual victim).
Victim has no right to appeal verdict.
No victim waiting room.
Treated like a piece of evidence.

1. Has no voice in court decisions, pleas, presentence, or sentencing.
2. Usually is not notified or present at time of sentencing.

1. Often unsatisfied with results of criminal justice system.
2. May fear retaliation.
3. Continues life with fears, damages, injuries, traumas.
4. Is expected to continue to support a system that treats him with less respect than the offender.

whether the criminal justice system should be invoked. Of the five hundred arrest situations, police and the court intake personnel exercised judicial discretions and prosecutorial discretions in relation to four hundred and eighty youths and the courts exercised those discretions in relation to twenty.

In practice, the pressures are on the police not to make an arrest unless they already have sufficient evidence to satisfy the district attorney with a good chance of conviction. Thus, "probable cause" or "reasonable belief" often becomes "the weight of evidence beyond a reasonable doubt" as a criterion for making an arrest. The result is that every day the police make decisions that properly belong in the courts, and by virtue of these decisions they deprive *victims* of their right to their "day in court."

Police discretion leaves it up to the policeman on the beat to decide whether the victim is entitled to justice. When justice is dispensed on the streets, more than half of all offenses are decided in favor of the offender.

Battered women especially suffer post-crime victimization by the police. Police are trained to discourage wives and girl friends from entering complaints against spouse or boy friends who have assaulted them. In cases of domestic quarrels the police will often pressure the victim not to make a complaint or demand an arrest. Several police training manuals advise police to avoid arrests if possible; to discourage arrests by advising women about possible loss of time, postponements, and the uncertainties of court appearances. Thus the police avoid making arrests and discourage the victim from seeking justice by reciting to them the difficulties they will face in court.

The procedure for handling domestic calls as detailed in the Police Training Academy in Michigan illustrates very well police reluctance to take any action in such cases:

    a. Avoid arrest if possible. Appeal to their vanity.
    b. Explain the procedure of obtaining a warrant.
       (1) Complainant must sign complaint.
       (2) Must appear in court.
       (3) Consider loss of time.

(4) Cost of court.
c. State that your only interest is to prevent a breach of the peace.
d. Explain that attitudes usually change by court time. .
e. Recommend a postponement.
   (1) Court not in session.
   (2) No judge available.
f. *Don't* be too harsh or critical.[3]

As attested to by the number of victims who fail to carry through in courts, judicial practices are discouraging enough, but to deliberately use them to discourage victims from seeking justice is tantamount to denying them their rights.[4]

In addition to the official sanction given to this practice, the sympathy of the police is often with the offender and not the victim. Susan Weiss, a Beverly Hills lawyer who specializes in battered women's cases, claims that doctors, lawyers, and policemen—not necessarily in that order—are the chief wife beaters.[5]

Police practice, if not policy, is not to take seriously the female victim's appeal for protection and to insist that the victim prove her allegations by waiting until she is attacked again before they will make any efforts to protect her. In these cases police discretion leads to sexist discrimination against female victims of assaults.

Police discretion is also influenced by class and ethnicity. The same crime committed by a middle-class White youth in suburbia is less likely to lead to an arrest than if it were committed by a Black, Hispanic or White ghetto youth. The police tend to treat all the youths of the ghetto as if they were potential offenders.

Is police discretion judicious? Obviously, a certain amount of discretion must be given the police. But when no arrest is made in half of the offenses, when sexism, racism, and class discrimination is rampant, when thousands of people are injured because of the failure of police to protect them, when the exercise of the option not to arrest often deprives the victim of due process and his right to redress of grievances, then police discretion is out of hand and some checks and balances must be designed. Even if racism, sexism, and class bias were eliminated, the use of police discretion would still be discriminatory unless victims had some way to appeal the decision of the officer on the scene. If the police refuse to make an arrest, the victim can make the arrest himself. But the laws regarding citizen's arrests are complicated, and citizens are not aware of their rights to do so.

Citizen's arrest is further complicated in some states by the requirement that the accuser take *physical* custody of the accused and deliver him or her over to the police. Considering the obvious fact that men generally outweigh women and are usually stronger as well, expecting the woman to take her attacker into physical custody is tantamount to preventing the arrest. If she could handle him, she probably would not need to call the police in the first place.

Susan Jackson dealt with the problems of citizen's liability and physical custody in citizen's arrest situations in a report on marital violence to the Women's Litigation Unit of the San Francisco Neighborhood Legal Assistance Foundation. She cited *People* v. *Campbell,* in which a citizen observed an attack, pulled the attacker off the victim, and then merely pointed the attacker out to the police, who then took physical custody. The court held that these actions constituted a legitimate citizen's arrest, even though the citizen neither physically delivered the accused to the police nor told the accused that he was under arrest. Jackson concluded, therefore, that a wife-victim should only be required to verify the offense, point out her attacker to the police, and say she wants to make an arrest. The police should then take him into custody.

At a public hearing in San Francisco, Jackson referred to a California statute that makes a police officer's failure to act upon a citizen's arrest a crime. She suggested that "discouraging" citizen's arrest would be covered under this statute, and that police officers could and should be prosecuted under it. And in a statement before the city's Police Commission, Jackson insisted that police should be required to inform all victims of their right to make a citizen's arrest.

Elizabeth Truninger suggests that if a woman is reluctant to make a citizen's arrest, she might press the charge of "disturbing the peace." Disturbing the peace applies to conduct such as threatening, quarreling, fighting, or even using "vulgar, profane, or indecent language within the presence or hearing of women or children, in a loud and boisterous manner." Since this crime occurs in the presence of police officers more frequently than instances of wife abuse do, arrest on this charge is, theoretically at least, more likely.[6]

Del Martin[7] reports that:

Police action is often designed to protect the department rather than the victim. For example, attorney Alix Foster told me that the Seattle police do encourage women to make citizen's arrests, but not necessarily for the purpose of bringing the man to justice. "In that way," Foster explained, "if ever an action for false arrest is brought, the police are immune from liability. The man would have to sue the woman." But Susan Jackson claims, with reference to this possibility that "police arguments that wives can be liable for a false citizens' arrest are disingenuous, since it is highly, unlikely that the wife will be mistaken as to her attacker's identity or as to the crime which has been committed against her."

POLICE PROTECTION

The ordinary citizen is compelled to depend on the police for protection against bodily harm and loss of property, and expects them to effectively insure the safety of the street and home against criminal incursion.

Where an offender appears to select his victims at random or on the basis of some idiosyncratic characteristic, such as young girls with blond hair, prostitutes, occupants of bars, and so on, the public is easily aroused because they feel vulnerable to an everpresent senseless and unknown danger.

But the majority of crimes of murder occur between people who know each other. People often think a "personal" crime is a personal matter and it is up to the persons involved to seek protection. The public is seldom aroused by family or lovers' quarrels that end up in murder or assault.

The police often minimize the danger of "personal" crime. They will ignore the battered wife's pleas for protection until she is assaulted and nearly murdered by an enraged boy friend or husband.

The police often advise an abused wife to apply for a restraining order to be served on the violent husband. The procedures for obtaining the order is complex and expensive, and once the order is obtained its value is questionable, to say the least. A restraining order can be acquired only after the victim has retained an attorney and paid costs for filing, unless she qualifies for Legal Aid. Filling out questionnaires, filing petitions, and anticipating court hearings are nerve-wracking ordeals in themselves. The woman may decide to abandon the whole thing once she finds out what is involved.

The prepared petitions must be filed with the court. If the order for the husband to appear in court is granted and if the woman does not qualify for Legal Aid, she must pay for the personal service of this order on her husband. The order must be served at least ten days before the day set for the hearing. The woman must then testify at the hearing to show cause—that is, to explain why the restraining order should be granted. These steps must be taken while the husband is still under no restraint and may be living under the same roof with the complainant.

Once the restraining order is granted, what can the woman do with it? "So she waves a piece of paper in his face and he thumps her anyway," a Legal Services attorney said to [Susan] Schwartz and [Dale] Mills [Seattle *Times* reporters]. If the husband threatens her again and she calls the police, they will tell her they can do nothing until he actually hurts her. If he does injure her, the police are likely to tell her that because the husband is under the restraining order, the matter is now civil, not criminal, and thus out of their jurisdiction. She will be advised to see her attorney and institute contempt proceedings.

Since instituting contempt proceedings is also a civil procedure, the wife must file *another* petition with the court to obtain *another* order for her husband to appear in court. And again, if granted the order must be served on the man (and paid for by the woman). At least another ten days will lapse before the court hearing, since the order to appear must be served ten days before, but court calendars being as congested as they are, even more delay is probable. If the husband is found to be in contempt, and if it is his first violation, he will probably be warned but not sentenced. If he does not appear at all, a body warrant may be issued and another court date set. And round and round it goes.[8]

Every individual has the right to expect that he is free of danger to his person and property in public and private places. He also has a right to expect to be protected when his person or property is threatened. He looks to the police to perform this function, since, ostensibly that is the purpose for which police departments were organized. In the division of labor in our society, the preservation of civic and public order and the protection of citizens is normally in the hands of the police. Under extraordinary circumstances that tax the limits of the police, the national guard or the army may be called on to take over this function. The use of the national guard and federal troops during strikes and the civil rights struggles are examples.

For the most part, police protection is viewed as protection of the public—not individuals. The practice of police protection is primarily a matter of protecting the "public" against civil *disorder*.

The protection of an individual who is not a significant public or civil figure is not considered to be an ordinary police function until he is actually robbed or assaulted. A person has to first suffer a violation of security before the police will come to his aid. The police will rarely recognize the direct threat of violence to victims as a legitimate reason to provide protection.

ATTITUDES TOWARD THE POLICE

Public ambivalence toward the police is widespread. Some fear and hate them, others admire and respect them.

The charge of police brutality and corruption has been substantiated often enough to create in many a cynical and suspicious, even fearful, attitude toward the police and their work. Every act of bullying behavior toward young people, every unprovoked threatening gesture, every unnecessary and overreactive brutal response on the part of the police reinforces the attitude among the public that as an organization, the police force includes a large number of people who are simply covering up their own sadistic and antisocial impulses. Of course, not all policemen are brutal and corrupt. Many dedicated and professional police officers function effectively even under the stigma of the public's image of the police. But in every occupation that performs the "dirty work" of society, there is an element of contamination and contagion. This is especially likely to be so in police work, because of the constant association with evil and wicked men and women, brutal and sadistic murderers, vicious thieves, incorrigible conmen.

Negative public attitudes toward the police reinforce their anxieties. That is one reason why a compensating subculture has been built up in which the police are the incorruptible providers of safety and protection against criminal behavior.

Morris and Hawkins[9] describe this subculture as follows:

> They huddle together, an anxious ingroup, battling the forces of wickedness, political corruption, citizen irresponsibility and decline in morals, particularly the immorality of youth. Their extra-corp contacts are cautious in the extreme. They are, they believe, insufficiently esteemed, inadequately rewarded, but gallantly carrying the burdens of society for a parsimonious and misguided citizenry.

This tension between the self-concept of the police and the public's image of them tends to differ in extent and intensity depending upon the volume of crime in a particular area. In large metropolitan cities with its high-crime areas, negative attitudes toward the police are likely to be intense and widespread. In the low-crime areas of the middle-class suburbs, attitudes toward the police are likely to be more benign. Likewise, in the high-crime areas the attitude of the police is likely to be more resentful and critical of the citizenry than in middle-class suburbs.

The police do, in fact, behave differently in these two environments. Less bullying of the youth, more courtesy toward the ordinary citizen, and a greater responsiveness to complaints and emergency calls are characteristic of police in suburban middle-class areas. Victims are often treated with more consideration, and the degree of post-crime victimization by the police is considerably less.

Many people are ready to blame police behavior for the high crime rate in metropolitan areas. Few people understand or are willing to acknowledge that a high crime rate is itself a cause of the kind of police behavior that results in an increase in the public's cynicism and disdain. Crime is a social phenomenon, not a police phenomenon. Its roots lie in the social fabric of our society—in the nature of our cities, with their provocative luxury adjacent to the poor living in concentration camps without walls; in the values of our economy, with its emphasis on status symbols, many of which have become to be regarded as necessities of life (people may not steal bread anymore but they will steal automobiles or TV sets, the new necessities); in the nature of our individualistic culture, with its disdain for unaspiring, unachieving human life; and in our overcrowded and overpopulated cities, which decrease the value of human life and increase violence and brutality.

A high crime rate tends to reinforce brutal behavior in the police. It is many times more dangerous to be a cop in a ghetto than in a peaceful suburban community. To be cautious, at times overreactive, at times bullying and rude, may under certain circumstances have survival value. The trouble is that under the pressure of police work in a high-crime area, the police tend to adopt this behavior as a general attitude whether the situation calls for it or not. The police, therefore, tend to view and treat all ghetto residents as potential offenders.

The police in large cities often function in a hostile environment because of the nature of the laws of our country. America is one of the few countries that attempts to legislate morality. Exploited and underprivileged people are not apt to hold the same moral values as the privileged classes in society. The line between oppression and enforcement is thin indeed. It all boils down to enforcement of what. Police enforcement of laws against victimless "crimes" (such as gambling, prostitution, and so on), which are viewed by many of the poor as legitimate and necessary ways to survive in the system, is seen as oppression. Thus, the view that the police are oppressive has a firm base in the values of the poor and underprivileged.

The tension between the police's self-concept and the public's image of them has also affected the way in which police react to victims of violent crime. Often their defense against the negative attitudes of the public is to "blame the victim." "You shouldn't have been walking on that street so late at night." "You shouldn't have been dressed so provocatively." "A decent person would not go into that bar."

The police more carefully treat those who may constitute a public nuisance, such as the mentally ill, or drunks. Police are trained in how to assist and deliver them to social agencies for help; this is recognized as a legitimate function of the police. But their attitude toward these sick and needy people is much different from their attitude toward victims injured by an offender. As long as an offender can be held responsible, the investment of energy of the police is toward him; the victim takes second place.

I think most police really would like to see something done for victims. They recognize the need. What they have difficulty with is how *they* can do it. They are usually willing to assist or cooperate with other organizations or services that assist victims. But they have a mental set. Their job is to deal with offenders, and having to bother with the victims is seen as an imposition, at times even an interference, with their primary task. The offender, not the victim, is the bread and butter of the police.

However, when the pressure is off, the police can be helpful to victims. A Bronx Senior Citizens Robbery Unit, the first to be created in the country, was recently inaugurated. The unit has earned an appreciative response from elderly victims, and Detectives Irvin Silverman and Bill Siegel have won the affection of many of the elderly. Elizabeth Griffith, an eighty-two-year-old victim of a savage beating and robbery, calls Detectives [Irvin] Silverman and [Bill] Siegel "my sons."

Recently she wrote the two men a letter of appreciation in her shaky handwriting. It reads, in part: "You two are so dedicated and have so much love and concern for the helpless old people who are like little lambs trying to survive in a den of wolves. There are so many muggers, purse snatchers and killers roaming the streets, we old people are not safe even in the day. We need thousands more like you to help clean up the jungle this city has become"[10]

And then there is Police Officer Richard Croce of the 48th precinct in the Bronx. He gives up one lunch hour a week to escort the elderly from the Mount Eden Center at 1660 Morris Avenue to nearby banks and stores. He also stops by the center several times a day on his beat. "These people lead such miserable lives," said the 27-year-old officer, who received a letter from Betty Ford commending him on his work. "They can't even walk out their doors, because they're such easy targets. And they can't even visit friends within their same building. That's how ridiculous it is. Can you imagine a life style like that?"[11]

These policemen have been assigned to do a special job—assist and protect the elderly and prevent victimization. They are as effective as can be expected under the circumstances, and are appreciated by those whom they help and know about their efforts. But the ordinary cop on the beat does not have the luxury of concentrating his efforts on one particular victim group. He is under tremendous pressure to respond to emergencies of all kinds. He tends to feel harassed and beset by inordinate and unfair demands on the part of his superiors and the public, and his behavior often reflects this. But when the police are given a specific assignment and freed from other pressures, they seem to do an effective job. Unfortunately, one cannot divide the police up into units for every possible type of crime or type of victim. Such "specialization" would result in organizational and administrative chaos.

POLICE TRAINING

A difficult problem for police officials is that of restricting the use of police tools to appropriate situations. In Austin, Texas, the sheriff of Travis County, Raymond Frank, dismissed a deputy because he admitted breaking "the cardinal rule of law enforcement" by hitting a man on the head with his nightstick.[12]

The law enforcement training that Texas officers receive includes strict instructions that the baton is not to be used on the head, the sheriff said. Because a suspect can be subdued by using the stick on other strategic parts of the body, "you accomplish nothing and you may seriously injure or kill the victim," according to a law enforcement class handout that the sheriff exhibited. A sheriff's patrolman said deputies are unhappy with the firing, and "what little morale we had has dwindled to nothing."

Here is a case where an attempt to restrict police use of their tools, while on the face of it plainly necessary, has led to a morale problem among the law enforcement personnel.

If tensions are so easily aroused, if police are so sensitive to restrictions to prevent abuse of nightsticks as control, will they not react similarly to restrictions on their use of psychological skills, which are much more subtle, more difficult to identify? The problem is not likely to be an issue in training police in the psychological skills necessary to manage family disputes but a growing practice among law enforcement agencies to teach police officers the psychological skill of hypnosis may pose serious problems when restrictions on its use are imposed.

Martin Reiser, head of the Los Angeles Police Department's Behavioral Science Division, is training police officers in the use of hypnosis[13] and the number of police departments across the country training their own personnel in hypnosis to interrogate consenting witnesses and victims in certain criminal cases is growing. Reiser has conducted at least two national training workshops in the use of hypnosis for law enforcement officers, which the Law Enforcement Assistance Administration of the Justice Department helped promote and nationally advertise. The purpose of such training is to elicit information from witnesses and victims to help solve a crime.

Hypnosis is an effective tool in extracting information from some people who are either unable or unwilling to remember. But it can also be a powerful technique to inject details that never occurred into a person's memory of an event. It therefore requires the most scrupulous professional responsibility and accountability. It would not be unlikely that a law enforcement officer, trained for one week in the use of hypnosis and under pressure to secure evidence, could even without realizing it suggest to the witness or victim certain "memories" that would be used as evidence. And it is possible that neither the victim-witness or the hypnotist-cop would be conscious of it. That is possible even under the best circumstances where the police officer is absolutely responsible and trustworthy.

But just as there are officers who under certain circumstances will unnecessarily strike a man over the head with a nightstick, there are some who will use hypnosis irresponsibly and to their own advantage, even to the harm of the victim. Hypnosis is a weapon that has traditionally been associated with the secret police of totalitarian countries.

Furthermore, the technique itself can be harmful to the victim-witness. The usual practice is to restore the memory of the criminal event by having the victim-witness "recall" it or "live through it again" under hypnosis. A characteristic of hypnosis is that memory is more improved if the hypnotized person "lives through" the original experience with all its emotional affect than if he is simply required to recall it. In other words, to maximize the success of the recall, victim-witnesses would be required to go through the emotional trauma of the crime itself. Such an experience, unless handled with professional care, can be psychologically damaging and lead to considerable pain and sufferlng on the part of the victim-witness. One has only to observe the traumatic emotional effect identifying the offender has on many to realize how catastrophic it would be to suggest the victim "live through" the experience again under hypnosis.

NEWS ITEM[14]

10 Rape Victims Identify Youth They
All Feared to
See Again

The young woman came haltingly into the room where the detectives and lawyers awaited her. She was instructed to approach the one-way window and to keep silent until she had viewed all six men in the lineup. One of them, she was told, might be the man who had attacked her.

She was one of 10 women who had come yesterday morning to the Manhattan District Attorney's office to try to identify a young man they all had prayed never to see again. She moved toward the window, spreading rings of perspiration on her light tan sweater, revealing the nervousness she had seemed bent upon controlling earlier, as she chatted in a hallway.

She stared as the first two men in the lineup came to the window for her inspection. Then, glancing toward the bench where No. 3 sat waiting, she gasped and began to scream. Her screams grew louder and her body shook so violently it seemed that she might fall. Two detectives rushed to help her to a chair as others stared in embarrassed silence at the floor, shifting from foot to foot.

"That's him!" she shrieked, before collapsing sobbing into the arms of her husband who had been summoned by detectives from the hall.

What is most curious is that even though police officials are constrained from using hypnosis on offenders, they seem to feel that it is perfectly all right for them to use it on victims. Even though the police claim that hypnosis will only be used on "consenting" victims, might they not feel that the victim who refuses to be hypnotized is hiding something. The law protects the offender from any part of police procedure that might force him to incriminate himself. But it does not protect the victim from being legally compelled to give evidence that may be embarrassing and self-demeaning, or that may result in considerable pain and suffering, even serious emotional trauma. This is just another example of how an offender-oriented criminal justice system is sensitive to the rights of the offender while treating the victim as a piece of evidence with no rights or considerations as a wronged person.

It seems to me that rather than training police officers to use hypnosis, psychologists and psychiatrists ought to protest its use.

Within the framework of an offender-oriented criminal justice system, there is constant pressure for the police to be exclusively concerned with the offender—to view the victim as an instrument for a successful prosecution. Yet the police are the branch of the criminal justice system that is in closest proximity to the victims. How they treat the victim is likely to affect the victim's attitude toward the entire criminal justice system. The magni-

Post-Crime Victimization

tude of unreported crime reflects the public's attitude about the criminal justice system in general and the police in particular. At least half the victims of violent crime consider it futile, even dangerous, to have any contact with the police. They expect to be treated callously, indifferently, and with concern only for the "law," which is often seen as lack of concern for them as a person. In the ghettos of the large metropolitan cities, it is street wisdom that the less contact one has with the police, the better. The attitude is similar to that of the young private in the army who soon learns to "stay away from headquarters." Avoiding the police seems more reasonable than seeking protection or assistance. And this attitude on the part of the victim leads the offender to believe that he can get away with criminal activities and that physical threats can be successful in restraining the victim from pursuing the matter. If he is successful, and he often is, the criminal is encouraged to try it again, very often on the same victim. The effect is a vicious cycle. Police attitudes lead to repeated victimizations, which in turn increase negative attitudes toward the police. This cycle must be broken—and it is up to the police to break it. There is considerable evidence to demonstrate that a victim-consciousness orientation—an attitude of caring and concern for the victim—produces radical changes in the attitudes of citizens. They want to believe that the police are concerned about them and they are appreciative when they see evidence of it. The following is a good example.

NEWS ITEM[15]

Two hard-eyed detectives in loose-fitting leisure suits (which tend to hide holsters the best) bent over Lily Stein in a lobby of Bronx Family Court the other day trying to reassure the distraught woman that the 15-year-old youth who had robbed her at knifepoint would not try to retaliate. Mrs. Stein, a nervous 64-year-old woman, seemed temporarily calmed. Earlier, she had sat sobbing and twisting her green and white wool stocking cap, saying to no one in particular, "Oh please, I can't sleep at night. Please, oh please. I'm trying to move out of that neighborhood." The woman, a resident of the South Bronx, had been brought to court by the two detectives from the Senior Citizens Robbery Unit, a two-year-old Bronx squad that works with the elderly victims of crime. She was there to identify her assailant, who had been arrested twelve times before for smaller crimes.

"Oh please, he lives in my neighborhood," she said of the youth who had demanded $200 from her at knifepoint in her apartment, but had settled for $129—which was all she had. "He'll come back and get me."

But after the detectives had reassured her that he would not and that the youth might have made repeated visits to rob her if she had not reported him, she made the identification. Then one of the detectives drove her to a Bronx real estate office where she looked at listings for a new apartment in a safer neighborhood.

This illustrates two significant aspects of police behavior that are different from the customary way police handle victims. First, the police provided the victim with transportation and an escort to court. Second, the detectives provided a meaningful demonstration of consideration for the victim by taking her to a real estate office. Such actions are rare in police handling of victim-witnesses. The reassurance of the police that the offender would not retaliate was important, but its veracity to the victim was immeasurably increased by the two detectives' attitude of personal concern. I am not proposing that every witness be provided transportation and a personal escort to court. But an obviously terrified victim-witness needs reassurance and live protection, not verbiage or promises. The demonstration of the serious intentions of the police to prevent revictimization—even if it is just helping her get to a real estate office to find a safer place to live—was important to convince this victim of their serious intentions to protect her.

It is not sufficient to simply *allow* a law enforcement officer to do these things; he should be indoctrinated with a victim-consciousness that produces them as a natural reaction in the course of carrying out his duties.

But raising the consciousness of police to the needs of victims is not sufficient to remedy post-crime victimization. Police indoctrination in victim-consciousness alone will not remedy established practices of the police system that routinely result in trouble for the police.

The Courts

Decisions that affect the lives of millions as well as those that drastically change the life—sometimes the life span—of an individual are made in courtrooms. To emphasize the solemnity of these occasions the atmosphere of the courtroom is deliberately imposing, dramatic, and frighteningly serious. The principal actors, the judge and the attorneys, are filled with a sense of self-importance supposedly equal to the weight of the decisions to be made. Every courtroom hearing or trial presumes to be a demonstration of the exercise of the awesome power of the state in an atmosphere of dignity, wisdom, and fairness. The architecture, the furnishings, the bench, and the jury box, the high ceiling, the solemn decor, all are designed to affect the atmosphere of a sacred chamber where significant decisions are made by dignified, serious, and wise people.

Perhaps in the Supreme Court the aura in the courtroom is a fitting context for the profound issues being adjudicated. But in the vast majority of cases in the criminal courts of metropolitan cities, the judicial process is a hollow mockery of all that the courtroom atmosphere is intended to produce. When you observe the behavior of the principal actors, you cannot help feeling that the "set" is a deception. The importance of the occasion, the dignity and solemnity of what is supposed to be taking place, and the wisdom and fairness of the process, all come off as a transparent charade to cover up a "production line" of criminal cases. Of course, the speedup is unfair to the offender. But an even worse characteristic of the haste with which cases are decided is the complete exclusion of the victim from the process. The game has one primary goal—to clear the calendar for the next case.

I sat on the judge's bench in Bronx Criminal Court and watched case after case being postponed or plea bargained— each hardly took more than ten or fifteen minutes—while the victim never was called, consulted, or asked to testify. Frequently, the victim was never told of the disposition of the case. Occasionally, a victim would remain in the courtroom for hours before discovering that it was all over. Postponements and plea bargaining are two of the most frequent causes of post-crime victimization.

Physical hardships, loss of income, as well as defeat of justice are routinely imposed on victims by the way postponements are permitted in criminal court. Victims whose cases get to court react with consternation and frustration at the unbelievably bizarre combination of Catch-22 rules, the administrative ineptitude—often deliberate—and the charadelike procedures that characterize the criminal court hearings and trials. It is commonplace for a victim-witness to appear in court, waiting as much as six hours and losing a day's pay, only to have a case postponed because of the lack of a report from the probation department or because the defendant's attorney claims he is not ready, or for some other administrative reason. The victim-witness is frustrated and angry about the physical hardship of sitting in court all day and the financial cost of losing a day's pay. Despite the anguish of unsettled action, he resignedly appears at the next scheduled date, only to go through the same experience—and the loss of another day's pay. The trial is postponed again for what appears to the victim to be the same reasons. This experience is usually repeated over and over again until the victim-witness gives up in disgust and fails to appear—at which time the defendant's attorney moves for dismissal.

In between postponements, the offender, free on bail, arranges to have his friends threaten the victim or in some cases, his attorney will pressure the victim to reduce the charges.

Post-Crime Victimization

A defense lawyer whose client is free on bail is able to manipulate time pressures to keep his client free. Typically he does this by pleading the client not guilty, by pretending that he is going to trial, or by creating scheduling problems and trial preparation burdens which cut into the time budget of the prosecutor. A number of the less reputable members of the private criminal defense bar are retained by their clients more for their known ability to "buy time on the streets" to keep their clients free on bail, than for their prowess in the courtroom. Some defense lawyers use ingenious technical stalls, even when there is no hope of acquittal, because they know old cases are settled more cheaply than fresh ones.[16]

The effect of these delays is to make the courts a partner with the offender in victimization.

Incidentally, the arresting officer is relieved from his usual assignment to appear in court. Thousands of patrol-duty man hours are lost by these frequent postponements.

Plea bargaining is the other most frequent cause of post-crime victimization by the courts. From a purely administrative perspective, the courts welcome plea bargaining. It speeds up the court process and relieves the pressure on the court calendar. The fact that it violates the constitutional rights of the offender is overlooked by both the courts and the legal profession. The Constitution proclaims that a person is presumed to be innocent until proven guilty. Plea bargaining, however, is based on a presumption of guilt. An offender is presumed guilty upon his say so. The only function of the court is to determine what he is guilty of and to fix the punishment.

But the very nature of plea bargaining is farcical. The offender is not required to admit or deny a charge of which he may or may not be guilty, but he is not "allowed" to deny a lesser charge which has not been proven and of which he may be innocent.

Plea bargaining is informal, institutionalized pressure on the offender to confess. It is unjust to the offender and it deprives the victim of an opportunity for justice. The victim of aggravated assault who has been crippled for life will not feel that justice has been done if the offender is sentenced on his admission to a misdemeanor. Worst of all, the victim is not even consulted about plea bargaining.

The usual plea-bargaining scene in the courtroom involves the defense attorney, the prosecutor, and the judge conferring at the bench. When they come to an agreement, the defense attorney talks with the offender to determine if he is willing to admit to whatever lesser charge is agreed upon in return for whatever sentence has been negotiated. If the defendant agrees, then a charade is acted out.

The judge inquires whether the plea is free and voluntary, and whether any coercion, threats, or promises were used to obtain it. To each question the accused makes the expected reply and the answers are solemnly recorded, although everyone in the courtroom knows that the plea has been arranged, that the realistic choices open to the accused are few and that the entire process up to that moment, from the structure of the penal code to the whispered assurances of the prosecutor and defense lawyer, has been structured to create threats and rewards leading to the plea.[17]

The judge, the prosecutor, and the defense attorney are all guilty of complicity in perjury. The witness does not understand how the offender can be sentenced without his testimony and is stunned to find the offender has been sentenced on the basis of a lesser charge. Since the arresting officer has participated in determining the original charge, and may have gathered the evidence to substantiate it, the judge will sometimes go through the formality of asking him if he agrees to the reduction of the charge. But it is only a formality—the prosecutor who formally makes the charge has been a party to the agreement. The victim is rarely asked for his comment.

The injustice of this procedure has created a wide demand for the abolition of plea bargaining. Most of these demands are motivated by a desire to see a harder line toward the offender. Certainly, in view of the injustices to victims, such an attitude is understandable. Barry Sudiker, president of Crime Victims Rights Organization in the Bronx, New York voices this attitude: "The politicians care more about murderers and the muggers than about the victims."[18] In detailing some of the demands of his organization, he included an end to plea bargaining and an end to lenient sentences for offenders. Sudiker also urged the restoration of the death penalty.

Several judges, responding to such pressures, have outlawed plea bargaining in their courts. But plea bargaining is still common practice in most criminal courts.

The struggle to end plea bargaining will be long and difficult so long as judges and lawyers are more concerned with the court calendar than with justice.

Many victims are mothers of young children; to appear in court they must secure a babysitter or leave them unattended. Even if they could afford a babysitter, many hesitate to leave their children with someone else, because frequently the offender or someone associated with him threatens to harm the victim or her children. Under such circumstances, mothers are often terrified to leave the house or allow their children to be on the streets or alone in the house. A mother who has been threatened is taking a heavy risk to leave the children to appear in court.

Most victims are completely unfamiliar with court procedure. In the courtroom they do not know what will be expected of them, and they are in awe of the judge and his powers, fearful of making a mistake that would put them, rather than the offender, on trial, feeling completely in the dark. There is no one to explain what is going on, what their rights are, and what is expected of them. Many victims have difficulty following the procedure in English. The offender, on the other hand, has his attorney to keep him informed of the status of his case and the proceedings.

These are some of the ways victims suffer from the administration of justice. Even the most humanitarian judges find it difficult to give more consideration to the victim. They are caught up in the pressures of the calendar, made worse by the incessant delaying tactics of attorneys. The legal profession bears its share of responsibility for post-crime victimization.

The Legal Profession

The legal profession as a group has been mandated and licensed by society to be the "guardians of justice." In exchange for that role, society has granted them the right to remuneration large enough to free them from the struggle for existence, high status, and autonomy over their professional conduct. In exchange for use of this knowledge and expertise, the ordinary citizen is expected to surrender control of the relationship, thus giving lawyers *authority,* the major form of power enjoyed by any professional in our society.

Because the lawyer deals with the casualties of society, people who by definition are in crisis, he is, as part of the social contract, given license to do dangerous things—peoples' lives and property are at stake—and to guard private, embarrassing, or dangerous knowledge. The legal profession has therefore built up an ethic and a system of rationalization for appropriate behavior, given the hazards and contingencies of their role. These have become part of the bargain between the lawyer and those he serves. The lawyer—like the doctor or other professionals who deal with casualties—does not permit the client to judge his competence or the quality of his work, and claims that such judgments must be restricted to colleagues—who perpetuate the fiction that all professionals are competent and ethical until found otherwise by their peers.

As a result the lawyer is placed in the position of someone who does not suffer the sometimes tragic or violent results of his own decisions. Others, who are dependent on him, must suffer the consequences of his ignorance, his mistakes, his self-deceptions, and his biases. C. Wright Mills[19] has labelled this "organized irresponsibility."

Everett Hughes[20] notes that wherever power is characteristic of one's assigned task, wherever one is doing something *for* or *to* someone else, the tendency to overuse it or even enjoy its overuse may be present. There are bound to be differences in perception, values, and judgments between those in crisis and those who presume to help. The legal profession jealously guards its right to define its mistakes and failures and refuses to accept complaint procedures or grievance mechanisms other than those controlled by lawyers themselves. Yet the innumerable tragedies of their mistakes and failures are part of the folklore of the world of offenders and victims. Because of the nature of their work lawyers are people who live by appearances, not substance. Guilt or innocence, bad or good, right or wrong, truth or falsehood are of no substance to them. These matter only in what they can be made to appear. The successful lawyer is one who can make wrong appear right, bad appear good, guilt look like innocence, and falsehood resemble truth.

Criminal lawyers are the natural enemies of victims. In their efforts to defend the person charged, the victim-witness is an adversary. They will spare no efforts to discredit the witness—make him out to be a liar, a cheat, or a fool. They will put a witness through severe emotional strain—break him down to a sobbing helpless creature if they could. The criminal lawyer who lets sympathy or compassion for the victim creep into his thinking is sunk. Consequently, lawyers have no interest in victims in criminal cases. They can't make a living that way. The state is not willing to pay for legal service to victims who can't afford to pay, as it is for the offender.

But in civil court cases some lawyers tumble over each other seeking the victim as client. They are more than willing to serve the victim in a suit that promises 30 percent of the award. This proves that lawyers do not have an inherent antipathy to all victims—only victims in criminal court.

The social system in which we now live treats knowledge and skill in human services as commodities, and assumes that they will be equitably regulated by the law of supply and demand in a free market economy. Today, professions are business enterprises, supplying for a price or withholding service. As such, the lawyer is an entrepreneur, and maximization of economic gain becomes his primary motive. The free-market philosophy applied to human services, as everyone knows, has resulted in the most needy having less service, of poorer quality. Left solely to the vicissitudes of the marketplace, the poor are without services, for there is a large enough and wealthy enough middle class to buy up all professional services including the legal services offered by lawyers. Only because the Constitution demands it do states supply legal services to the offender without means, and only in criminal cases. If they are poor, both the complainant and defendant in civil cases and the victim in criminal cases are left without any legal services.

NEWS ITEM[21]

COLEMAN ASSERTS BAR FAILS PUBLIC

Charges It With Neglect of Clients Who Cannot Pay High Expenses

By Lesley Oelsner

Atlanta, Aug. 7—Secretary of Transportation William T. Coleman Jr. accused the organized bar today of having "failed the American public" by turning its back on people unable to afford high-priced lawyers.

He referred to both poor individuals and citizen groups seeking to assure that the "public interest" is taken into account in governmental decision-making.

Mr. Coleman, speaking at the American Bar Association convention here, said it was the job of a lawyer to "represent everyone who comes in and has a cause." But he said that "the organized bar has gotten away from this" with the development of huge law firms and high hourly fees.

And government, he said, "is not particularly sensitive to demands and needs," other than those represented by "special interests."

Ralph Nader, addressing the same audience, complained that there was "a new wave of complacency" in the legal profession about public interest law, a sense of satisfaction because there had been at least some progress in that area in the last few years.

Mr. Nader, the consumer advocate and a long-time critic of the legal profession, contended that the progress was nowhere near enough. "Most people," he said, "are shut out of their own legal system." Chesterfield Smith, a former president of the American Bar Association, differed somewhat with the other speakers' assessment of the organized bar, saying that the bar could be proud of what had been done. He too called for much more support from the bar, though, and suggested two changes in particular: a system of dues going to public interest law; and a change in the profession's ethical canons to require at least some public interest work by each lawyer. "You need someone who can represent the general interest," he said.

The Constitution insists that every offender has the right to be legally represented in court even if he cannot afford it. The criminal justice system and the legal profession have devised a number of ways to comply with this requirement. The public defender and legal aid are two of the most widely used at the present time.

Since the defendants requiring legal aid are from the low socioeconomic strata and cannot afford to pay for an attorney, the lawyers offering their services are usually young, just graduated from law school, who volunteer because they see this as an opportunity to gain valuable experience and hopefully build a reputation. The defense of offenders who come from the ghettoes and are destitute is considered "dirty work" by the more experienced and respectable lawyers. They tend to leave this work to the recent graduates, rationalizing it as providing them the opportunity for "valuable experience."

Most of these young lawyers come from comfortable middle-class homes and all that they know of ghetto life comes from the newspapers, television, or the movies. The closest that they have ever gotten to the seamy side of life is what they have been able to see on the streets as they pass through on their way to school, office, or home. Poor people all look alike to them. No wonder that in the drudgery of dealing every day with cases of assaults, thefts, and muggings, victim and offender become hardly distinguishable. Neither the victim nor the offender are seen as persons. To the young lawyers, they are to be processed. Using the poor for training purposes is a coveted opportunity and a long-standing practice of law and medicine. The criminal justice system expects it of them. The legal profession encourages them.

What kind of deterrent can punishment be if the guilty offender is led to believe that he can "get off with a bargain"? What kind of justice is the victim experiencing if he is informed that the offender "got off with a bargain" without his ever being consulted? Such experiences only serve to increase the victim's fear of the offender and are generalized to the criminal justice system and the legal profession as well. The victims see the role of the criminal justice system more as a "collaboration" with the offender than as a deterrent. They see the legal profession as playing a game with the criminal justice system rather than acting as the guardians of justice for the public. And today it is true that the term "guardians of justice" is nothing more than hollow rhetoric.

Recently, I was invited to participate in a symposium on plea bargaining. One of the other participants was a well-known criminal lawyer. During the discussion, a minister in the audience took the floor to remark about the injustice of the process of plea bargaining. He accused lawyers and judges of perjury each time they engaged in plea bargaining. The lawyer responded to his accusation of injustice as follows: "Anyone who thinks that the criminal justice system dispenses justice is naive." When the minister questioned him and asked, "Is it not true that the lawyers and judges are committing perjury each time they practice plea bargaining?" the lawyer responded with, "Well, I think perjury is a little harsh. I would say it was a charade." I mention this not to make an *ad hominem* argument against plea bargaining, but simply to cite an example of what I have continuously observed—the cynicism of the legal profession. It seems to me that lawyers, whose social mandate is to be the guardians of justice of our society, are expected to operate on the principle that if the criminal justice system does not dispense justice, then it is their responsibility to demand that it does rather than cynically accept the failure of the system and operate within that framework.

Lawyers are granted an elite status in our society in return for which they are expected to protect the individual--whether criminal or victim—from injustice. Some distort this mandate to mean their role is to protect the offender from punishment, even if that punishment is justifiable on the basis of a fair trial. And the offender's rights have been carefully safeguarded. An offender has no right to escape punishment just because he can "get away with it." Many lawyers, however, operate on the principle that their job is to help the offender get away with it. In the fantasies of young law students this is the most exhilarating experience of law practice. What a paradox! The young law students learning to be the "guardians of justice" are aroused to a high state of excitement by the fantasy of getting an acquittal for a person charged with murder. The missionary zeal of rescuing someone who is innocent is not what excites them—the guilt or innocence of the person charged is immaterial. The thrill lies in the exercise and confirmation of their cunning and craftiness. Young lawyers see themselves as gladiators. That is their ego-ideal. The victims of ancient gladiators were animals or other gladiators supposedly of equal strength. The victims of modern legal gladiators are the offenders and their helpless victims.

While the large body of guarantees of the rights of offenders was formed to secure for the offender the benefits of the institution of criminal justice, the guarantees are used by the legal profession, with the collusion of the courts, to gain illegitimate advantages.

The legal profession, then, is guilty of trying to turn the advantage of a cherished value of the public to illegitimate self-interest which, in the long run, defeats the purpose of the cherished value to begin with. The success of offender attorneys in subverting the social and judicial aims of the criminal justice system has the effect of encouraging offenders. It contributes to the causes and extent of crime in America and in part is responsible for the failure of the criminal justice system to make any headway in preventing crime. Crime prevention will be a hollow mockery so long as the offender knows that he can convert society's cherished values of justice to protect himself from the consequences of his criminal activities.

Furthermore, the police and court's lack of responsibility to victims reinforces the offenders. The offender begins with an attitude of *un*responsibility to the victim. If society in general and the criminal justice system in particular demonstrate no genuine interest in the violence done to victims, the offender's original attitude is encouraged. If society is not serious about abhorring violence, the offender is encouraged to use it for his own selfish interest. It is old folk wisdom that violence begets violence. But that is only a half truth. Violence against the strong begets violence, but violence against the weak begets fear. The sophisticated habitual violent offender is well aware of this. Consequently, his victims are the weak, the handicapped, the elderly, and the poor. Against these, he can be violent, sadistic, and scornful. When he comes to court, it is to his interest to be sly, cunning, and deceitful. The interests of the victim, the aggrieved party, is to be straightforward, open, and honest. If he is, it is likely that the offender's behavior will be more successful than his. There is probably no other place in our society than in the courts, except perhaps in politics, where slyness and cunning are rewarded more than straightforwardness and honesty.

The moral obligation of society to victims as well as to offenders is on the agenda today. A new social policy with the victim as the central focus is necessary. A proclamation and explication of the rights of victims is needed to stimulate criminal justice policies and procedures to place in balance the rights of the victims with those of the offenders. It is the victim, rather than the offender, who is more often the victim of injustice today.

I would be remiss if I did not mention that, unlike most other countries, a majority of legislators in this country are members of the legal profession. They bring to the legislative process many of the attitudes acquired as lawyers. That is one reason why it is so difficult to get legislation passed to aid victims of violent crime. Volumes of legislation have been enacted by offender-oriented members of the legal profession to assure the rights of offenders. Legislation assuring the rights of victims—recognizing the justice of making the victim whole again—often meets with the same indifference among legislators that one finds among lawyers.

The Human Services Agencies

Only the poor know the teeth-gnashing, tongue-biting sense of frustration of dealing with the human service agencies. Indifferent to human feelings, unresponsive to human suffering or need, degrading in its attitude toward its "supplicants," the big bureaucratic apparatus is manned by men and women who are compelled to act like programmed robots in an atmosphere of frozen frenzy—where despite a great deal of hectic activity time creeps at an imperceptible pace. This is the setting for post-crime victimization by the human service agencies.

The halls of city hospitals are filled with ravaged or battered and bruised bodies identifiable only by the nature of their disability. John Davis is not John Davis but "the stab wound in Room Seven." Mrs. Cohen is not Mrs. Cohen but "the fractured pelvis on Ward C." Each bed is a cold, compartmentalized chamber where the internal and external parts of the patient have been disassociated from the human being they comprise and become the sole identity of the person.

In the waiting rooms (so aptly named) of the public assistance, social security, and unemployment agencies Sara Clark is not Sara Clark but case number 104-16-5945, a faceless, sexless, colorless, humanless identity. Everyone is treated regardless of need or suffering in the same equally indifferent, by-the-numbers fashion. If loss of a place to live caused by fire can be considered an emergency why is the same loss caused by criminal vandalism not considered to be in the same category? Senseless and bewildering rules, regulations, and practices, designed for administrative convenience—without regard for the consequences to people—repeatedly revictimize the victims of violent crime. The language spoken is a hash of bureaucratic gobble-degook and is droned in automatic tones from the mouths of robots. "It will take six weeks to process your check." (More nearly ten if you're lucky and live that long.) "Come back on Tuesday and we'll give you an appointment then for two weeks from Friday." Why does it take six weeks to process a check? At least thirty-five days must be administrative *indifference* time.

Paul Smith, the victim of a mugging and stabbing, returned to his apartment after two months in the hospital to find the utilities shut off, an eviction notice, and his car impounded. His unemployment check was stopped because he was unavailable for work. He has no money for food. He is desperately in need of emergency financial aid and applies for an emergency check at the welfare department. They inform him that he may make a routine application for welfare but he is not eligible for an emergency check because the regulations of the welfare department only recognize emergencies caused by fire, flood, or earthquake. He is eligible for welfare but they cannot waive the ritual of delay because his desperate need was caused by a fellow human being, not by God.

Mrs. Bertha Reed lives in a small apartment and manages to live frugally on her Social Security check. Many other tenants in the house are also elderly people living under the same conditions. On the first of the month, the mail boxes are ripped open and her Social Security check is stolen. At the Social Security office Mrs. Reed is informed that it will take about six weeks (why is it *always* six weeks?) for the check to be replaced. If

Mrs. Reed had cashed the check and the money was stolen it could be replaced in about two weeks. How's that for Catch-22?

These cases are fictitious composites of cases processed by the Crime Victims Service Center. They represent the typical responses of the agencies when representing victims in the circumstances described.

How the human service systems rip-off victims when aid is made available is illustrated in the following from a report of the New York State Crime Victims Compensation Board:[22]

Many hospitals in our state continue to find imaginative ways of recovering money from this Board. More and more common are bills sent to victims from hospitals for emergency care treatment and from the physicians working in these emergency rooms, both for the same services.

Further, in some cases not only do these staff physicians bill for the same services rendered and billed for by the hospital, but the charges submitted were exorbitant. On the advice of this Board's examining physician, we have generally compromised each bill with the creditor-doctor for many hundreds of dollars less than the amount originally billed. Nevertheless, it is generally understood that we overpaid in these situations.

Some hospitals are charging us exorbitant "handling charges" for abstracts of medical records and photocopying of medical records when we request them. A few hospitals are even charging this Board a fee for a copy of the hospital bill rendered to its patient.

Other hospitals billing us for services rendered by them in their emergency rooms also bill us for the same identical services of "attending physicians." Once called "staff physicians" and paid for by the hospitals, these "attending physicians" now receive no salary from the hospitals but are given their own private office, secretarial help, etc. and are paid for by their involuntary patients, [victims]. In a typical case we investigated, we learned that the "attending physician" was listed as the "personal physician" in the so-called "voluntary operation" after going through an "emergency operation" in the hospital. The bill from this doctor for services rendered was a high one and yet the patient [victim] never remembered meeting this doctor nor did he know this doctor was listed as his personal physician.

In still other recorded cases, physicians who had extensive Medicaid patient practices now advise their patients [victims] to make claim on this Board since we would pay 100% of the bill whereas the doctor would have to accept a substantially smaller amount as payment in full for services rendered under Medicaid.

The belief that aid to victims is primarily a matter of expediting by referral the victim's contact and application with the appropriate human service agency serves as the basis for most victims' assistance programs. But the most frequent need of victims, emergency financial aid, is not available in the human service system. The system is not responsive to the "emergency" nature of the situation. The need, therefore, is not one of *expediting* processing but of changing system policies and regulations to make emergency aid for victims possible and available. Until such changes are made, victims' assistance programs will be largely ineffective and post-crime victimization will continue to frustrate the victims of violent crime.

CHAPTER 5

A BILL OF RIGHTS FOR VICTIMS

Victims of violent crime in the United States are not only victimized by criminal offenders, they are also the victims of an archaic criminal justice system. The scales of justice are unbalanced, heavily weighted on the side of the offender. Historically the criminal justice system has emphasized its sensitivity to the rights of offenders. Thus an offender-oriented criminal justice system has accumulated a large tried and tested body of law that attempts to protect any person charged with a criminal offense from miscarriages of the law. This emphasis on legal justice for the offender has resulted in discriminatory and oppressive practices against victims. The struggle for legal justice for offenders has produced social injustice for the victim. While guaranteeing the rights of persons charged with a criminal offense, our body of law has neglected the rights of victims. Perhaps neglect is the wrong word, for it is not simply a matter of neglect or insensitivity to victims but rather an orientation—a mind set that the concern for criminal justice is primarily a concern for criminals. It does not seem to occur to experts in the criminal justice system that the system ought to be as concerned with the rights of victims as it is with the rights of offenders. Rather, most members of the criminal justice system feel they must protect the criminal and guarantee him justice from the natural reaction of vengeance of the victim.

How can a criminal justice system that doesn't even recognize the victim as a victim concern itself with victims' rights? Since victims are only witnesses, they are subject to the rules of testimony designed to protect the offender. Victims will remain an oppressed minority until the criminal justice system is compelled to change its present concept of its role in society and acknowledge that every person who commits a criminal act not only violates the laws of the state but also violates a person. *Every criminal act involves a breach of law and a person wronged. The duty and obligation of the criminal justice system is to rectify both these acts, not to ignore the person wronged and deal exclusively with the breach of law. Witnesses are not simply testimentary objects; they are persons who have been wronged and as such have certain rights.*

The legal and moral obligation of the state is to maintain an orderly society—to guarantee every person who has been criminally wronged by another not only the means of seeking redress for his grievance in the form of punishment for the offender, but also that the person wronged will be made whole again. I use the phrase "to be made whole again" to mean that every person who has suffered injury or loss due to a criminal act has the guarantee of the state that he or she will be restored to whatever condition of life existed before the criminal act. Upon that fundamental concept I am proposing a bill of rights for victims. Basically what that philosophy implies is that no citizen of the United States shall be required to bear the burden, either physical or financial, of a criminal incursion upon his body or life situation. It is an assumption that ought to be part of every society that aims at maximizing social justice. No society that claims its purpose is to regulate the orderly conduct of living can be socially just as long as it permits innocent citizens to bear the burden of criminal assaults on their lives.

A Bill of Rights for Victims

Punishing the perpetrator is a reactive form of justice. It is based entirely on the concept of deterrence. Deterrence, as we all know, is not working very well. Behind the concept of deterrence is a definition of the problem of crime as a matter of stopping people from breaking the law. That is a narrow, unbalanced, and legalistic definition of the problem. Crime is a social problem, not merely a legal one, and the definition of the social problem changes with the social situation. Crime is a changing social problem depending on the nature and extent of crime under particular social, economic, and political conditions. The crime problem today is not only the problem of high levels of criminal activity, but high levels of the most nefarious, sadistic criminal assaults on the elderly, the poor, and the middle classes. Under today's social conditions, a major question is: "What is the role of a just society with regard to its citizens who have suffered a personal wrong through a criminal act? Until this aspect of the crime problem in the United States is considered and changes made in the criminal justice system, there can be no justice for victims of violent crime. The system will remain archaically offender-oriented, continue to victimize the victims of violent crime, and continue to be guilty of post-crime victimization.

I am not naive enough to believe that as soon as a statement of victims' rights is formulated, the system will then respond with serious effort to implement it. Our American bureaucracies are gung-ho innovators, but damn poor implementors. Considerable active public support and pressure will be required to get the various components of the criminal justice system to even consider these reforms, let alone implement them. An aroused public outcry and the aid of enlightened public officials is necessary to put victims' rights on the agenda of criminal justice system reform. The following statement of victims' rights puts the issues before the public.

THE INVISIBLE VICTIM

Victims' Bill of Rights

1. Every citizen of the United States who suffers injury or loss from a criminal act has the right to be made whole again as a matter of social justice.

2. Every citizen of the United States who suffers injury or loss from a criminal act shall be considered by the criminal justice system primarily as a victim—a person who has been criminally wronged. Status as a witness to a criminal act shall not result in neglect or subrogation of a victim's rights as a criminally aggrieved party.

3. Every victim of a criminal act has the right to immediate emergency financial, medical, and legal aid.

4. Every victim of a criminal act has the right to protection by the police and courts from any threat, coercion, or improper persuasion.

5. Every victim of a criminal act has the right to equal protection under the law, including the constitutional right to remain silent and the right to be represented by an attorney of his or her own choosing, or a victim's advocate appointed by the court.

6. Every victim of a criminal act has the right to participate or be represented, and exercise concurrence or nonconcurrence, in all plea-bargaining decisions.

7. Every victim of a criminal act has the right to the immediate return of all personal property recovered by law enforcement officers.

8. Every victim of a criminal act has the right to complete and up-to-date information regarding the investigation and prosecution of the perpetrator.

9. Every victim of a criminal act has the right to hold law enforcement officers legally responsible for their own negligence or poor judgment.

To implement these rights of victims, certain changes in policies and practices are necessary. In the following section are a number of proposals for reform of the policy and practice of the courts, the police, and the human service systems. Since I am not an attorney my approach is not a legalistic one. These prescriptions are not offered as laws but as social policy proposals. I am sure there will be those who will object to these reforms on legal grounds. My position is simple. These reforms are proposed because I believe they are socially necessary to insure a greater share of justice for victims of violent crime. The rationale for these reforms is not legal but social. Fundamentally, they are motivated by a desire for a more socially just criminal justice system. If legalistic realities stand in the way of these reforms, then the system should be changed to remove the obstacles.

Court Reform (Policy and Structure)

Basically, court reform needs to be directed to shifting the judicial process from its present offender-oriented view of the victim as an instrument of the prosecutor for presenting evidence of a crime against the state, to recognizing the victim as well as the state as the aggrieved party. It must modify some of the more flagrant offender-oriented policies and practices that legally victimize victims and institute new policies that reflect the rights of victims.

To eliminate the present obstructionist policy requiring the victim who desires to be made whole again to sue the offender in civil court, I suggest the following changes in criminal court procedures based upon and excerpted from those made by Schafer[1] for the British Criminal Justice System. These recommendations are just as appropriate to the American criminal justice system.

Criminal trials shall be conducted in two parts: The function of the first part shall be to determine guilt or innocence. The second part shall consist of the sentencing procedure in which the victim may testify to what is required to make him or her whole again.

1. Restitutions to the victim of crime should be entertained within the scope of the criminal procedure by the same criminal court that deals with the criminal case, and the sentence should be a combined one, of which restitution should be a part.

2. Restitution may be claimed by the victim, but in default thereof, the court should deal with restitution as part of its duties.

3. If the question of restitution may cause considerable delay in deciding the sentence so far as ordinary punishment goes, the court should pass a part-sentence concerning this latter and should postpone the deci-

sion of restitution. In such a case, the criminal court should entertain the question of restitution after passing this part-sentence without delay and should couple the previously passed part-sentence with the decision concerning restitution.

4. A decision on restitution should state the amount of restitution and order the amount of installments as a percentage of the offender's earnings, to be paid by the offender during his stay in the penal institution and afterward during the period of probation, or after he has paid the fine if this be the only penalty. The decision should be based on a consideration of the offender's social position, personal circumstances, and reasonable but minimal standard of living.

5. With the aid of fines or other sources of revenue, the state should set up a compensation fund, and victims should be compensated from it when the total amount of reparations necessary turns out to be irrecoverable, or if the offender is not known. This makes it possible, and standard procedure, to impose restitution on the offender as part of the sentence of the criminal court.

I am not suggesting that this restitution will be a successful means of making the victim whole again. It does, however, make the offender participate—to whatever extent is realistically possible—in the process of restoring the victim to his precrime status. The judge or jury in the sentencing procedure can assess the extent of injury or loss to the victim as well as the extent to which the offender can realistically be expected to make restitution.

Restitution also introduces into the criminal court procedure a recognition of the victim as an injured party and shows the offender that the court will not only punish offenders for breaking the law but will insist that anyone who criminally takes something from someone will have to give it back—even if restitution takes years and requires that the offender's life be organized around the task of repaying what was taken. Anyone who criminally injures someone is responsible for the cost of restoring the victim to normal health. If it is seriously practiced, such a message to offenders may be psychologically more effective than simple punishment in the form of incarceration.

This policy also suggests a different philosophy for the corrections system. Jail should be the place where the offender's daily life is organized and supervised around the task of making the victim whole again. Ideally, sentence length should depend on the time necessary to make the restitution determined by the sentence of the criminal court. This is a more humane and psychologically sound procedure than the present myth about the purpose and function of the prison system.

The procedure I propose will institutionalize in the criminal court process the concept that the victim as well as the state is an aggrieved party and the concept that the function of the criminal court is to determine guilt or innocence and to render a just resolution for *all* parties involved, that is, for the offender, the state, and the victim.

PLEA BARGAINING

The procedure just outlined may be subverted by the practice of plea bargaining, where the charge and sentence are negotiated before the trial takes place. To prevent this subversion, I propose that the victim participate in the plea-bargaining process. So long as we have plea bargaining, the victim should have the right to participate. For example, the fact that the victim would agree to a lesser charge if the offender pays back so much per month gives the victim leverage to bargain for restitution.

However, the victim, though he participates in plea bargaining, does not have the power to enforce restitution. I propose, therefore, that the practice be established to give the victim "sign off" power, which means the victim has the right not to concur in what has been agreed upon. That right has no enforceable consequences, except that the judge would take the victim's nonconcurrence into consideration before he passes final judgment on the case.

LEGAL SERVICES

The Constitution insists on free legal services to offenders without means; no such services are provided victims. That the prosecution provides the victim with whatever legal services he requires is a false assumption—mere rhetoric, an empty theoretical abstraction. In practice, prosecutors consider such demands on the part of victims as impositions that interfere with the pursuit of the case as a crime against the state. Yet every victim has the right to equal protection under the law. Since the law provides a public defender for offenders, and since prosecutors do not provide victims with needed legal services, I propose that victims have the right to request that the court appoint a victim's advocate whose duty it is to plead the cause of the victim with respect to all of his rights.

The advocate would represent the victim in plea bargaining. Many victims become emotionally upset when they come face-to-face with the offender, especially in rape cases. Rather than compelling them to suffer another emotionally traumatic experience, the victim's advocate would represent their interest in plea bargaining.

If restitution is to become part of the sentencing procedure, the victim's advocate would represent the victim's interest in determining the amount or manner of restitution.

The idea of an ombudsman or advocate is not new. The difficulty with implementing the concept is largely a matter of providing a power base that makes it possible for an advocate to have some clout when pleading a cause. An advocate appointed by the court would have the power of the court to back him up just as a probation officer currently has. While he would have no enforcement power, his position as an arm of the court would give the advocate sufficient stature to make an official record of his plea for the cause of the victim. Putting the victim's view on the record for the judge or jury to consider would be a great step toward a more balanced criminal justice system. It would fill a gap too long empty by giving the *victim* his "day in court."

There are numerous other functions a victim's advocate can perform, and I will cite them under the appropriate victims' rights discussed.

A Bill of Rights for Victims

I have discussed those rights of victims that require reforms in the policies and functions of the court. The prescriptions I have suggested address themselves to the problem of how to change the court system to provide a legal mechanism to make the victim whole again as well as provide the victim a vehicle by which he can be recognized as an aggrieved party and have his grievances heard, considered, and adjudicated within the criminal court processes.

The other rights of victims vis-à-vis the court do not necessarily require policy or structural changes in the criminal court system but can be dealt with by changes in the current practices of the criminal court.

POSTPONEMENT

One practice that can be changed is the abuse of postponements. Postponements are, with few exceptions, at the discretion of the judge. The routine abuse of postponement by defense attorneys is often allowed because judges, sensitive to the offender-oriented philosophy, consider it proper to be lenient and afford sufficient time to defense attorneys to defend their case. Attorneys are aware of the propensity of judges to be lenient about postponements. Any sophisticated defense attorney knows that the longer he can delay the trial the better the chances of the offender—evidence gets stale, witnesses' memories fade, public sentiment subsides, prosecutors' motivation weakens, and victims give up hope of ever seeing a conclusion. Furthermore, judges are often relieved of the pressures of the day's court calendar by granting postponements. Putting off the trial to another day may be administrative relief to judges but it is post-crime victimization to the victim.

With regard to postponements, the argument is made that delay in concluding a case is less objectionable than the consequences of precipitancy. The point is not valid, however, for precipitancy is not always the alternative to delay. A case with one or two postponements is most unlikely to involve precipitant action. Frequently, postponements occur not out of a desire to avoid precipitancy but out of a strategy to use delay to circumvent the process of justice, to win dismissal or better terms in plea bargaining. In these circumstances—and they constitute most cases—delay results in pressure on the victim to quit the case or to agree to anything to bring it to a close. Given the situation in the courts today, the issue in most cases is not delay or precipitancy, but the abuse of delay to deprive the victim of his quest for justice.

If postponements were simply an administrative matter caused by difficulties in getting paperwork done on time, I am certain that procedures could be designed to remedy the situation. For example, the first time a case is postponed for want of certain papers, a high-priority tag with a time limit could be placed on them. The postponement could be granted with a firm deadline instead of an estimate leading to a series of postponements until the papers appear. A limit of one postponement based on a reasonable estimate of the time needed to make the paper available would have several desirable effects: the physical and financial hardship on the victim would be reduced; the use of postponements as a strategy to wear down the victim until he gives up would be minimized; and the practice of using repeated postponements to buy "street time"—the time the offender is free on bail—would be discouraged.

In some cases, additional postponements may be necessary if the defense attorney does not have the required papers twenty-four hours before the scheduled hearing or trial. Then the victim should be notified in advance of the intention to postpone. Having received such notice, the victim need not appear in court and a motion for dismissal would not be allowed. After the first postponement, further postponements would not be allowed in any subsequent hearing or trial, unless such previous notice has been given to the victim-witness.

The need for a court-appointed victim's advocate is clearly indicated here. The advocate can plead the cause of the victim before the judge to prevent interminable and abusive use of postponements.

As mentioned before, one of the costs of repeated postponement is that of having the arresting officer relieved from his usual assignment to appear in court. It is difficult to estimate the amount of money that could be saved by requiring twenty-four hours notice for motions to postpone. It could be in the millions. Even excluding the financial savings, however, notification of postponements would at least provide thousands of additional man hours on patrol duty.

Such changes in the practice of postponement would speed up the court process without denying the offender any of his rights, while at the same time giving consideration to the rights of victims.

Victims would be more inclined to cooperate with the prosecution if the court could provide a day-care or nursery program for young children while the victim is in court. Such a court program could be organized by one of the family social work agencies. Or the program could be organized under the Department of Welfare and financed by the federal day-care program.

Whatever the system, some victim-witnesses will fail to appear at a hearing or trial where postponement is anticipated. Some dismissals will occur due to their failure to be available to give testimony, but the procedures I propose will drastically cut the number of cases where victims give up because of post-crime victimization by court procedure.

Since the victim-witness is assisting the criminal justice system in prosecuting the offender, he should not be penalized financially by losing pay. Victims should be reimbursed for "time lost at work" because of court appearances. Such reimbursements can be made through victims compensation boards.

These prescriptions will not do away with post-crime victimization by the court system. They are remedies that will alleviate

121

some of the injustices, provide victims minimum resources necessary to get a "fair shake" in court, and minimize the negative reactions to post-crime victimization by the criminal justice system.

Police Reform

Two basic issues of victims' rights require police reform. They are (1) the question of police discretion, and (2) the issue of police protection. Here are my proposals for police reform. (See also the section on post-crime victimization by the police, pages 76 to 95.)

POLICE DISCRETION

Every victim should have the right to appeal the discretionary decisions of the police and the district attorney. If the police, exercising their discretion, fail or refuse to make an arrest, there is currently no mechanism by which a citizen can appeal. The only recourse a victim has is to make a citizen's arrest. A citizen's arrest, however, is often difficult, especially if the police refuse to cooperate, and it often may place the victim in jeopardy. Besides, given the history of vigilantism in this country I am reluctant to recommend the broadening of the powers of citizen's arrest.

Of course, a more victim-conscious court and police would result in greater consideration being given to the grievances of victims in cases where police exercise discretion.

In some instances, citizens have a right to appeal police action or reaction to a citizen's review board. These have always been resisted by the police, and their effectiveness is highly questionable. But somehow the police ought to be held accountable for their decisions. Some states have granted immunity to their employees for any negligence or mistakes in judgment made in the course of their duties. In many cities the police cannot be sued even if their decisions result in great harm to a victim. There are other cities, however, that are leading the way in making their police and other employees accountable to their citizenry. Austin, Texas, for example, has just financially indemnified all of its police officers and has withdrawn the municipal immunity formerly extended to them. That is a step in the right direction. It provides a mechanism for victims by which they can hold police officers responsible for their discretionary decisions and offers a way for victims to be reimbursed for any damages resulting from such decisions. One or two successful suits will quickly make the police more careful in exercising discretion. I propose that every law enforcement officer shall be covered by malpractice or malfeasance insurance and shall not be protected by municipal, state, or federal immunity.

POLICE PROTECTION

I have seen victims—particularly battered women and the elderly—whose entire life styles are organized by terror. They live in seclusion, hoping their unsafe apartments wlll provide them the minimum security necessary to keep alive. They will not leave their apartments even during the day to do necessary food shopping unless accompanied by someone they know. They never go out after three o'clock in the afternoon, when school lets out. Their homes are literally prison cells. These people have been the victims of physical attack, and the offender has threatened them with further harm if they report the crime to the police or if they prosecute. If the victim does inform the police of the threat, he learns that the police rarely recognize a direct threat of violence as a legitimate reason to provide protection. A threatened person has to first suffer an attack before the police will come to his aid.

Sometimes the police will advise a threatened victim to secure a protection order. But a protection order is a piece of paper. It is not a defense against physical attack. It may have some deterrent value, but the distinction between deterrence and protection is meaningless to victims who are paralyzed by fear and feel they need to be defended against imminent physical attack.

If the police were required to provide twenty-four-hour protection to every threatened victim, they would have little time for anything else. However, existing practices with protection orders, as I have already pointed out, demand a degree of self-mobilization that is unreasonable to expect from people paralyzed by fear, and are ineffective as deterrents because for the most part they do not carry the authority of the criminal courts.

I propose the following reforms in the procedures for protection orders to strengthen their deterrent effect and provide victims with some reassurance that the police and courts take seriously the threat to their person and are doing something.

1. A victim who has been threatened may make a complaint to the district attorney's office and ask for a protection "warning." The D.A.'s office will investigate the complaint and if justified issue a warning to the perpetrator, putting him on notice that further threats or acts will result in a protection *order*.

2. When a protection order is issued, it is to be delivered to the perpetrator by the police. *Violation of a protection order would be considered a felony.*

3. If a protection order is violated, no plea bargaining shall be permitted either on the violation or the original charge.

Here is another instance in which a victim's advocate could be useful. An advocate could advise the victim of the procedure, follow the process, assuring that each step is properly carried out, keep the police informed of any attempted violation, and in the event of violation follow through with the district attorney in prosecuting the violation as a felony.

Giving protection orders the teeth that they need will considerably lower the possibility of revictimization.

Making the offender more aware of the person he has wronged will certainly increase his awareness of the role the victim is playing in getting him punished. In some cases this might result in offenders making greater efforts to threaten or discourage the victim from prosecuting. The criminal justice system that becomes sensitive to victims' rights must develop procedures to protect the victim from any attempt by the offender to discourage the victim from pursuing his rights and playing an active role in securing justice for himself. Undoubtedly, in some cases, making the criminal justice system more victim-oriented will result in making the offender more victim-oriented in his efforts to escape the consequences of his criminal act. Protection for the victim becomes even more salient in a victim-oriented criminal justice system.

INFORMATION

Every victim has the right to full and complete information regarding the investigation and prosecution of the perpetrator. At present the common practice is to keep the victim uninformed, sometimes for months after the trial is completed. Here is an excerpt from letters to the editor of a daily newspaper.[2]

I was a rape victim in Houston three years ago. After two lineups— the last one successful—I waited one year to be informed that the man who raped me was indeed in jail. This was only after many calls to the D.A.'s office and even more days and nights of knowing nothing. Was he still free? Did I identify the right one? Was he still after me? All these thoughts are hard to contain and spill over into a person's life. I didn't want him dead or castrated but I did want him in jail.

The anguish and anxiety of not knowing is clearly evident in this victim's letter. It is typical not only of rape cases but of most cases of violent crime.

I propose that the community relations officer of the police department be charged with the responsibility of securing and providing to the victim any requested information about the progress of the case. If the case goes to trial the victim's advocate can keep the victim informed and make certain the information is made available.

THE INVISIBLE VICTIM

RECOVERY OF PROPERTY

A common form of post-crime victimization by the police is the manner in which recovered stolen property is handled. In many instances victims have been unable to get their property back even though it has been recovered, as it is retained by the police as evidence. This could mean a delay of six months to a year or longer—until the trial is completed. Afterward the administrative procedure for return of property is so cumbersome and time-consuming that often victims give up trying. In some cases the time elapsed is so great that the victim has already replaced the stolen property and does not bother to recover it. In many cases victims have their last penny stolen. They have no money for food or for rent. The money recovered by the police is retained as evidence, for months—sometimes years—while the victim and his family suffer. It would be a simple matter for the police to certify that the recovered property belongs to the victim, return it, and at the trial present the certification as sufficient evidence that the property was found in the possession of the offender.

Again the victim's advocate can make the certification to the satisfaction of the police and court. It seems senseless for the police and court to penalize the victim and compel him and his family to suffer while his money is locked up in the recovered property bins of the police department.

I believe much of what I propose will work to the advantage of the police and the victim, if the police would demonstrate a more active and visible concern for the rights of victims. A program of indoctrination in victim consciousness in police training academies is an absolute necessity if the police are to increase public support and cooperation. A victim-conscious police force would soon see an increase in reports of crime and a more cooperative and appreciative attitude among those more commonly victimized. The Senior Citizens Robbery Unit of the Bronx is an example of how negative attitudes toward the police are turned into respect and deep appreciation. Police authority is not weakened by an attitude of concern for and service to the victim.

Human Service System Reform

Our crime victims service in the Bronx showed that the priorities of the needs of victims of violent crime were: emergency financial aid; emergency medical services; and legal services. In short, they needed money, a doctor, and a lawyer, and they needed it now! But emergency financial aid is not available except from churches and other charitable organizations. In many cases victims are reduced to an indigent state by the crime. As a result they are treated as though they are welfare clients. They are not. Abe Simon, the Director of Victims of Crime Aid League (VOCAL), is a heroic volunteer worker for victims' rights. He is constantly frustrated by the rules and regulations of the various social service organizations. Much of his volunteer's energy is spent in trying to deal with agencies that look upon his victim-clients as welfare supplicants and not as citizens with the right to be made whole again.

The elderly who are especially vulnerable to victimization require special programs addressed to their needs. Elderly women and men are targets for violent attack and robbery far out of proportion to their percentage of the population. Here are the factors that increase their susceptibility to attack:

- Many older people live alone.
- Many are in poor health, and an older person too weak to run away or resist is a prime target for attack.
- Many of our elderly live on fixed incomes, which restrict them to residing in low-income neighborhoods where crime levels are high.

- Many older citizens are in rent-controlled apartments and are unable to find and afford comparable living quarters in safer neighborhoods.

- Many aging citizens are reluctant to report crimes for fear of reprisals. This reluctance to go to the police makes them particularly vulnerable to revictimization.

- Physically, many old people never recover from the effects of a beating or violent attack. Recuperative abilities decline with age, and an injury that heals in a younger person often remains a lifelong ailment for an elderly person.

Immediate crisis intervention following a violent crime can do much to help the person cope with his or her fears and anxieties, which might otherwise linger for years.

Another element of an elderly victim program must be prevention. Information on personal safety and on security devices should be distributed to the elderly, but great care must be taken not to place too heavy an emphasis on the effect that individual elderly citizens or senior citizen groups can have in preventing crime. The police have developed sophisticated multimedia crime-prevention presentations; however, there is little evidence to support the effectiveness of many of the suggested techniques. I do not mean to imply that crime prevention efforts by elderly individuals and groups should be abandoned. But the police cannot blame crime victims for their misfortune because endorsed crime-prevention methods are not followed. The real responsibility for protecting the aged still remains with local law enforcement officials.

New and innovative efforts must be made to develop effective crime-prevention programs for the elderly. Self-help programs such as tenant patrols and instruction in self-defense do not appear to be suitable for senior citizens. Perhaps door-to-door escort services providing protection during shopping trips and elevator operators employed to escort the elderly from the elevator to the safety of their apartments are the kinds of services most needed to safeguard older people.

A Bill of Rights for Victims

People living on fixed incomes suffer serious loss at the theft of even a small amount of money; and the procedures for recovering or being reimbursed for stolen Social Security funds are cumbersome and inadequate for meeting the crisis that results from theft.

I propose the development of a credit card system for the aged to eliminate the need for carrying cash or Social Security checks and thus eliminate the stolen funds or checks problem. Credit cards would be issued on request to each individual and Social Security funds deposited into each person's bank account monthly. Senior citizens would no longer receive the actual checks, and thus would not be such good candidates for theft. The Social Security Administration will, upon request, send a person's check directly to his bank each month. Aside from some small amount of cash for cigarettes, movies, or transportation, the elderly can write checks. Sometimes merchants are reluctant to accept checks. Often credit cards are more acceptable to merchants—they involve less risk—and credit card slips can be deposited in the merchants accounts as easily as cash or checks. Computer technology already in use by banks and credit card companies would make implementation of such a program immediately practical.

The idea that victims have the right to be made whole again is directed at the attitude that they are welfare supplicants. Victims should not be viewed with the same prejudiced stigma as other welfare clients usually are. No welfare client should be stigmatized. But the classification of poor victims, or those reduced to poverty, in the same manner as other welfare clients implies that victims are unworthy "chiselers" trying to get something for nothing. The idea that the victim should be made whole again is a totally different rationale for giving aid than the concept that society should take care of the poor as a matter of grace. Victims of violent crime are no less victims and no less needy than victims of natural disasters. They are entitled to the same consideration without any lessening of status. Once the federal government confers disaster status on a group of victims, it directs all social service agencies to extend their benefits to them without delay. Victims of violent crime should also be granted "disaster status."

I propose that: (1) the federal government direct all social service agencies receiving federal funds to extend disaster status to victims of violent crime; (2) all benefits extended to victims of natural disasters by these agencies be extended to victims of violent crime; (3) victims of violent crime who have emergency needs have the right to go to the "head of the line" for immediate attention. To expedite the processing of these emergency cases, a selected number of staff members of these agencies should be trained as emergency expeditors to process the claims of victims of violent crime.

No less an authority than Supreme Court Justice Arthur J. Goldberg[3] in the preface to a symposium on victims of violent crime in 1970 stated that victims of violent crime should be treated with the same consideration as victims of floods and hurricanes. It is, Goldberg claimed, "especially appropriate in the light of the responsibility which society must bear for the crime itself. Crime is, after all, a sociological and economic problem as well as a problem of individual criminality." He reminded the audience that "what the equal protection clause of the Constitution does not command, it may still inspire."

CHAPTER 6

RESTITUTION AND COMPENSATION*

Laws, principles of justice, and social policies are, in the final analysis, based on some concept of human nature. In the early centuries of human existence, before law as we understand it today was developed, customs and rituals regulated the behavior of the members of the community. When these customs and rituals were invested with power—the ability to mobilize the resources of the community to enforce them—they became laws. The substance of these laws was determined by basic assumptions about human nature and the means necessary to control human behavior.

Revenge is sweet. The primitive emotion it expresses is alive and well and living in all of us today. Taken for granted as an intrinsic characteristic of human nature, revenge historically has accounted for two major practices for achieving justice—public and private vengeance. In public vengeance, man's propensity for vengeance was projected onto the gods, deities, spirits, and other

---

* I am indebted to Glenn B. Martin for his analyses of the various state programs. He worked closely with me as research associate while researching State Crime Victims Compensation Laws in preparation for a master's thesis at the Lyndon B. Johnson School of Public Affairs, University of Texas at Austin.

forces of nature. Believing that man was vulnerable to them, the community as a whole moved to protect itself from vengeance it believed was caused by individual members defying or provoking the spirits. Thus the fear of vengeance became the motive behind certain tribal laws.

In very simple societies the only offenses with which the whole community concerns itself are those which are held to risk a *common* injury from this supernatural vengeance—such as ceremonial offenses, breaches of the tribal marriage laws, witchcraft, and especially murder by witchcraft, and so forth. . . .

Even in the case of murder the interest of the community is far more eager than any mere concern for the sanctity of life could explain. Where we find public action against homicide it often appears on closer inspection that the gods, or spirits, or earth herself, refuse their help to man until the pollution of shed blood has been atoned for.[1]

Community guilt or responsibility for the wrongdoer was commonly accepted. The tribe as a whole risked disaster if it did not violently disassociate itself from the wrongdoer by making expiation for the unholy act. The "doctrine of the right of the community to punish"[2] evolved from the ancient tribal belief that the violation of taboos brings catastrophe on the entire tribe. Therefore, the tribe has the responsibility to punish the offender to expiate its guilt.

The fear of revenge also stemmed from the belief that certain individuals who had been wronged by a member of the community could invoke the spirits to avenge them by punishing the wrongdoer. The "dread of a supernatural vengeance" lasted well into the Middle Ages. It still exists today among some African tribes.

Several years ago I had the opportunity to visit Nigeria as a consultant to the Behavioral Science Institute of the University of Ibadan. During my short stay I visited Aro village, an experiment in mental health treatment, where mental patients were being cared for by the native villagers under the direction of medically trained personnel. I was fortunate to be permitted to participate in a group discussion by patients about the causes of mental illness. Many of them felt their illness was caused by an "enemy"—someone whom they supposedly offended. Seeking revenge, the "enemy" had convinced the spirits to enter the patients and punish them by making them feel strange sensations and causing them to behave in strange ways. While some of them felt unjustly punished because they were innocent, they all accepted the idea that a person wronged had the power to enlist the spirits' aid to inflict punishment on the wrongdoer.

Private revenge is the other earliest form of vengeance. The principle of "an eye for an eye and a tooth for a tooth" guided the conduct of all who were personally wronged. Considered a sacred duty of the victim or his nearest relative, this kind of vengeance led to the blood feud, which was responsible for vendettas spanning several generations. The danger of clan or family extinction by the vendetta eventually led to the substitution of the blood price for the blood feud.

The idea that reparations should satisfy a need for vengeance appears first among the early Greeks of the Homeric period. Homer tells us in the *Iliad* that Agamemnon took from Achilles his woman Brisies. This made Achilles furious, and he refused to help Agamemnon in his struggle against the armies of Troy. Agamemnon offered to return Brisies and to pay a large sum of money to atone for the wrong he had done. Achilles refused. Agamemnon then sent a delegation to Achilles, to ask him to relent and to assist him in the battle. In the *Iliad,* Aias chastises Achilles, who remains unrelenting in his anger against Agamemnon.

"Cruel man! A man will take blood price from one who has killed his brother or his own son; the slayer remains in his own country by paying a heavy price, the other controls his heart and temper after accepting the price; but you are implacable, your temper is merciless, such is God's will—and all for one girl."[3]

Of course, this had only the sanction of custom and was not law. There was no way Achilles could be compelled to accept reparations.

With the development of large city-states, voluntary reparations were supplanted by specific tariffs or legal reparations to be paid. An early example of this is found in the Code of Hammurabi, which prescribes both punishment and reparations. Here we find the first recognition of the state's responsibility for making the victims or their families whole again.

The Code of Hammurabi specifies in sections 22 to 24:

> If a man has committed robbery and is caught, that man shall be put to death. If the robber is not caught, the man who has been robbed shall formally declare what he has lost ... and the city ... shall replace whatever he has lost for him. If it is the life of the owner that is lost, the city or the mayor shall pay one maneh of silver to his kinfolk. [4]

As the power of the state increased, it demanded that part of the compensation levied on the offender be paid to it in exchange for maintaining the peace (between the victim and the offender). In addition to paying reparations to the victim, the offender paid a sum to the state that guaranteed the offender no further vengeance from the victim.

In Saxon, England, the *Wer,* the payment for homicide and the *Bot,* the compensation for injury, existed alongside the *Wite,* the fine paid to the king or overlord. [5]

As the state monopolized the institution of punishment, the law became divided into criminal and civil law. At about the end of the Middle Ages, violent crime against a person became a crime against the state. The state became the one that was wronged and demanded all of the reparations in the form of imprisonment and in fines. The person that was wronged was left to the exigencies of the civil courts to seek justice on his own.

> It was chiefly owing to the violent greed of feudal barons and medieval ecclesiastical powers that the rights of the injured party were gradually infringed upon, and finally, to a large extent, appropriated by these authorities, who extracted a double vengeance, indeed, upon the offender, by forfeiting his property to themselves instead of to his victim, and then punishing him by the dungeon, the torture, the stake or the gibbet. But the original victim of wrong was practically ignored. [6]

Restitution and Compensation

The history of justice reveals an interesting dialectic. In the beginning crimes were considered personal wrongs and the laws provided the means by which the wrongdoing could be righted, either by reparations and/or punishment. The idea of justice was focused on the problem of justice for the victim, the person who had been wronged.

In medieval times the idea of justice was twisted from its original meaning—justice for the victim—to its present focus on concern for justice for the state. The perversity of the progress of criminal justice robbed the victim of his historic entitlement to an equal share of justice. Our criminal justice system is still operating on this medieval theory of justice.

This brief historical review illustrates a progressive development from private vengeance to state control of vengeance. The state also abrogated to itself—through the criminal justice system—all forms of restitution or compensation that formerly were considered the right of victims. This development can be summarized as follows:

1. The phase of private vengeance.
2. The phase of voluntary "compositions" [compensation] for crime, offered and accepted instead of vengeance.
3. The phase in which the community specified a tariff of legal compensations.
4. The phase of the repression of crime by the state, private vengeance no longer being tolerated.[7]

We must remember that this transformation is very gradual; the different stages often overlap each other; and it is not only for homicide, but for other wrongs suffered by the individual, that the community gradually takes over retaliation from the private citizen, the principle of revenge, hitherto sacred, gradually (perhaps imperfectly) giving place to a respect for public justice, or at least a fear of the penalties.[8]

Social justice today demands that what the state has taken away it must give back. The principle of justice asserting the right of victims to be made whole again and the obligation of the offender to the victim as the aggrieved person needs to be reasserted. The victim expects moral reproach of the crime, and in addition, he expects the state to compel the offender to make reparations to satisfy his desire for revenge.

The state, when dispensing criminal justice, does not fight against legal phantoms, but against the acts of living human beings. The object of punishment is not merely to grant citizens the pleasure of participating in a ritual restoration of law and order. The modern criminological approach to punishment will not tolerate retribution, but it must not neglect the victim's interests. While punishment must lose its retributive character and lean towards giving the criminal a chance to work his passage back to society, it must on the other hand make the criminal sentence in some way beneficial to the victim.[9]

Restitution

Today court-ordered restitution is a popular proposed remedy. Stephen Schafer[10] says that restitution takes three different forms. One of these is the finelike restitution or compensatory fine, generally known as *Busse,* which appears mainly in the German, Swiss, and Mexican legal systems as well as in the laws of some American states. It is, essentially, a monetary obligation imposed upon the offender as an indemnity to the victim, and is in addition to the ordinary punishment imposed by the criminal court.

Another form restitution takes is similar to *Busse,* but the court need not restrict its award to the actual damage suffered by the victim and may require the offender to pay a greater sum of money, up to double or treble the value of the injury caused by the offender's crime. This again can be found in the laws of some states. Its punitive nature is evident from the extent to which the award is not restricted to the actual loss but may exceed it to the victim's benefit.

In the third form restitution is substituted for criminal proceedings, or at any rate for punishment. It appears in this guise in the laws of some states. Where the offender performs his obligations to indemnify the victim, the criminal proceedings may be closed and the offender discharged without punishment. By allowing restitution in lieu of punishment, the criminal law here becomes closely interwoven with the claim of the victim to restitution.

But restitution, payment by the offender to the victim for loss or injury, is not a viable instrument to make the victim whole again. On the other hand, compensation, payment by the *state* to the victim for loss or injury suffered because of a crime, is not an effective means of getting the offender to realize his responsibility to the person he wronged. Social justice requires both restitution *and* compensation.

Restitution cannot make the victim whole again because most criminals do not have the necessary economic means. Ninety percent of convicted criminals have annual incomes of less than $5000 at the time of arrest. Over half of all convicted felons are unemployed at the time of arrest. Forty-three percent of all persons tried for a felony have court-appointed counsel because they are judged to be indigent at the time of arrest.[11] In addition the corrections system has so far failed to provide the convicted offender with the opportunity to earn sufficient money to make meaningful payments to the victim.

A victim may sue an offender in civil court to recover his losses. To do so, he must pay for his own attorney, and he is further victimized by additional loss of time from work. Victims know that most offenders are poor and an award arising out of a civil action alone will probably be worthless to them. Even in the rare instances that the victim has sufficient resources to bring a civil suit against the offender, the number of criminals who are convicted and possess sufficient assets to satisfy a civil judgment against them is far too small to consider civil action a suitable means for repaying victims.

The idea that a victim must still establish a legal right to restitution even after the offender has been found guilty and sentenced to prison is unjust and unfair. Furthermore, since only an average of about 15 percent of reported violent crimes result in convictions, and assuming that all those convicted are able to earn enough to pay restitution, that would still leave 85 percent of the victims of violent crime unrecompensed. Add to that the fact that 95 percent or more of the offenders would be financially unable to pay restitution, we are left with the harsh reality that under our present system more than 99 percent of the victims of violent crime would be unable to collect restitution.

Restitution is not, therefore, an effective victim aid program. Its value lies not in its effectiveness in helping victims but rather as an instrument to make the offender more conscious of his debt to the *victim*. Also, it gives the victims a sense that the criminal justice system recognizes a personal wrong was done. "To the offender's pocket, it makes no difference whether what he has to pay is a fine, costs, or compensation. But to his understanding of the nature of justice, it may make a great deal." [12] Theoretically, it would be most beneficial to the offender and the victim if the offender *could* make restitution. But given the present situation, to insist that reparations be the offender's responsibility would simply increase the victim's post-crime victimization.

Justice in human relations requires the offender be held responsible—and participate to the best of his ability—in making the victim whole again. But to rely solely on the offender to indemnify the victim is to penalize the victim. Under these circumstances it is the state's obligation to see that justice is done—and victims compensated for injury and loss—while simultaneously insisting through the criminal courts on the offender's responsibility to the victim and determining how much of his resources are to be allocated as restitution.

Compensation

Because of the failure of civil suits, private insurance, and restitution as methods of assisting victims of violent crime, the concept of compensation by the state has rapidly gained favor.

Already, twenty states have enacted compensation laws (see pp. 156 to 159), and the Rodino bill* now before Congress obligates the federal government to reimburse those states that have crime victims' compensation laws up to 50 percent of the yearly cost of the program. No doubt, given sufficient support from the public, this bill will pass Congress. As a result, many other states are expected to follow with legislation to aid victims.

Among the states, the laws are by no means uniform. They differ in rationale, in the amount of benefits, in eligibility requirements, and in other characteristics. All of them have crucial weaknesses, which result in their helping only about 1 percent of victims. Despite their weaknesses, crime victims' compensation promises to be the most effective means of relieving victims of the disaster of victimization. An analysis of existing crime victims' compensation laws would provide invaluable aid to those presently considering such legislation in the various states, for it could prevent the repetition of some of the shortcomings of existing state boards and present recommendations for amending existing legislative policies and practices to make them more effective.

No two state victims' compensation programs are totally alike, but many share common characteristics. Laws authorizing public compensation to crime victims usually establish a commission or board that investigates claims and authorizes the payment of benfits to victims. However, some states assign victim compensation to a preexisting agency, such as the Workman's Compensa-

*See note 17, p. 204.

tion Board. Eligibility for public aid is restricted to those injured in an unprovoked criminal attack and to "Good Samaritans" injured while attempting to prevent a crime or assisting a law enforcement officer.

Eligibility varies from state to state; however, in every state the victim is required to promptly report the crime and cooperate with law enforcement officials. Other requirements concern his or her financial position, number of dependents, and employment status. If the victim satisfies all the criteria for eligibility and applies for state compensation, he—or the survivors—can be compensated for loss of earnings and reimbursed medical expenses. These awards may consist of either lump-sum payments, protracted awards involving periodic payment, or death benefits for the victim's dependents. All programs prohibit double recovery—the compensation benefits are reduced by the amount of other public or private insurance benefits.

RATIONALES

There are three popular rationales for victim compensation: citizens' rights, welfare (public assistance), and social insurance. The concept of citizens' rights maintains that the state has a moral obligation to protect all citizens and to make reparations if the protection fails. The welfare justification, like any welfare program, is based on the concept that a merciful society should assist citizens in need as a matter of grace. The third concept considers the state as a superior risk bearer, and is comparable to worker's compensation.

CITIZENS' RIGHTS AND THE ABSOLUTE DUTY OF THE STATE.

This rationale is seldom the basis for state compensation. Police protection, in a democratic state, cannot extend into people's homes and families. And, yet, arguing that the state has an absolute duty to protect requires just that: an omnipotent and omnipresent police law enforcement agency. Consider the statistical information about crime. The Federal Bureau of Investigation's

Restitution and Compensation

Uniform Crime Reports indicate that nearly one-fourth of all homicides are committed by relatives of the victim. The President's Commission on Law Enforcement and the Administration of Justice[13] reports that 20.5 percent of male and 46.1 percent of female victims of assault crimes are victimized in residence. Police protection cannot possibly extend to all personal relations and into all homes. If it did it would pose a threat that would outweigh the value of compensation to the victim. Police authority would extend into the areas traditionally thought of as beyond public control, for example, the family. Protection provided by the state can be less than absolute and still include the concept of victim compensation. "Absolute duty" does not seem an appropriate rationale for victim compensation.

WELFARE.

Modern society now provides public assistance for the sick, the aged, and the unemployed. The rationale is offered: Why shouldn't society assist innocent victims of crime?

Few states openly acknowledge victim compensation as welfare, but as long as the aid is based on need, that label is inescapable. Although it is rarely stated as such, this rationale forms the basis of many existing programs. State victim compensation with a paupers' oath requirement is welfare.

It seems to me that crime victims' compensation should not be considered a "handout." Judge David T. Bazelon[14] of California remarks that state criminal injuries compensation based on welfare ". . . is an attempt by the well-fed to feed the hungry in a very unfriendly fashion, as if the giver might at any moment change his mind and gobble the morsel himself."

Not all crime victims have low incomes. While it is true that the majority of violent crime victims have small incomes, crime is not exclusively aimed at these groups. The uninsured, middle-income person also feels the sting of enormous medical bills or loss of earnings resulting from victimization. The dilemma faced by the middle-income group is not limited to matters relating to state crime victim compensation; individuals in this rather ill-defined group experience problems with other governmental assistance programs as well. Not poor enough for public assistance, they still face indigency when struck by catastrophe. Medical indigency, for the middle class is an iatrogenic social disease of our health-care system.

SOCIAL INSURANCE.

The third major justification for aid to crime victims draws certain parallels between victim compensation and worker's compensation. The rationale for worker's compensation insurance is the inevitability of industrial accidents and the difficulty an injured laborer has in recovering damages. One legal scholar explained the difficulties of the employee at common law: "Once injured, the worker has no effective right to redress, for the law favored his employer who called upon one of the 'three wicked sisters of common law'—assumption of risk, contributory negligence, or the fellow servant rule—for his defense." [15]

The rapid industrialization of American society made necessary an administrative remedy to the injured worker outside the common law. In a similar fashion, the rising crime rate makes necessary the fashioning of an administrative remedy for victims of crime outside the boundaries of the common law. The industrial revolution called for special governmental adaptation to worker's needs; the crime revolution requires similar governmental action to meet the victims' needs.

I have two serious objections to the concept of victim compensation as social insurance. If such programs are considered a form of insurance, then someone has to pay a premium. In Workman's Compensation the employer pays the premium. Who will pay the premium for every citizen of the nation? There is no justice in compelling employers to do so. And even if that is done, who will pay the premiums for the unemployed? Should every citizen be required to pay an insurance premium to receive the right to be made whole again when victimized by an offender?

Restitution and Compensation

Many statutes passed by legislatures first offer a declaration of policy or purpose. In the case of victim compensation laws, these introductory statements note what led legislative bodies to adopt such programs. Some programs do not adhere to the rationales given in the preamble. For example, few declarations of purpose mention that the statutes establish welfare programs, and yet many programs can be viewed as such. Many programs mention the absolute duty of the state to protect the citizens against crime as a justification for their existence; but the actual operation of the program reflects a welfare orientation. The majority of state victim compensation programs are operated like welfare programs, despite their high-sounding rhetoric.

Enactment of the first victim compensation laws was initially triggered by a desire to compensate "Good Samaritans" who were killed or injured when they came to the aid of others. In New York City on October 9, 1965, Arthur Collins was stabbed to death when he came to the aid of two young women who were being molested on the subway.

Reacting to media publicity about the incident, three months after the Collins murder the City Council passed a "Good Samaritan" statute providing up to $4,000 for any person injured or killed while attempting to prevent a crime on a public street or in a public transit system facility. The council also sent a resolution to Governor Nelson Rockefeller requesting consideration of a state compensation program for innocent victims of violent crime. The New York State Crime Victims Compensation Act was signed into law on August 1, 1966, by Governor Rockefeller.

Maryland's compensation law was also motivated by a "Good Samaritan" incident in which a milktruck driver was murdered while attempting to prevent a crime. The Maryland law was proposed to the State Legislature in 1966. The legislature hesitated to enact this innovative program. However, after a delay of two years, the bill was finally signed into law on May 7, 1968.

While serving as captain of the Honolulu Police Force, Governor John Burns of Hawaii became familiar with the plight of victims of crime. Based on his police experiences, he strongly supported a state Criminal Injuries Compensation Act. The first attempt failed because legislators feared the costs of the program. When the maximum award per victim was revised downward from $25,000 to $10,000, the legislature approved the bill.

In 1972, a Seattle, Washington, woman suffered paralysis as a result of a gunshot wound. The victim, Mrs. Pat Hemenway, testified in support of a crime victims' compensation measure from her wheelchair before a committee of the Washington state legislature. It took over two years for the Washington legislature to approve a crime victims' compensation act. Mrs. Hemenway died before the legislation was enacted. To accommodate her dependents, the lawmakers provided that the act be retroactive to July 1, 1972. Receiving nearly unanimous support from the legislators in Olympia, Governor Daniel Evans signed the bill into law on June 5, 1974.

Unlike the states noted above, no dramatic motivating incident preceded the enactment of victims' compensation legislation in Alaska, Kentucky, Michigan, and Virginia. The Alaska victims' compensation bill became law in July 1972; Kentucky's passed in 1975; Virginia's and Michigan's in 1976. At the present time, a total of twenty states have enacted some form of victims' compensation legislation.

How effective are present crime victims' compensation laws? Not very. Comparing the number of reported crimes in 1976 with the number of awards made by some of the states, we find that New York made awards to 0.9 percent of the victims of violent crime. In Maryland only 1.9 percent of the victims received compensation. In Washington state, 4.5 percent of the victims were helped, and in Kentucky, 1.3 percent of the victims received assistance through crime victims' compensation. If we consider all twenty states that already have crime victims' compensation laws in existence, the average number of victims who are helped by these compensation programs amount to approximately 1 percent. In the face of such great need, why do these programs help such an insignificant number of victims?[16]

One major reason for the low utilization is the attitude of victims themselves; the other significant reason is the restrictions and obstacles of the programs that tend to discourage victims from applying. Restrictions, obstructions, and lack of information amount to a form of bureaucratic rationing that enables the administrators of these programs to keep their costs at a minimum. While it is politically expedient for a state to proclaim that it compensates victims of violent crime, it is also politically expedient for the administrators of such compensation programs to minimize utilization and thereby reduce the costs of the program.

I have already discussed how victimization itself produces an attitude that discourages the victim from seeking assistance. The traumatic experience of a violent crime produces a state of hopelessness and an inability to cope that makes it difficult for the victim to mobilize inner resources to do anything to help himself. It sometimes takes months for a victim to recover sufficiently from the traumatic experience to make any effort to seek assistance. The welfare philosophy of many programs also produces in many victims a reluctance to seek help. Victims are reluctant to declare themselves paupers in order to be eligible for assistance. Also, poor and economically deprived victims tend to think of themselves as people victimized by life; victimization by an offender is accepted as the human condition. And, finally, the cynicism toward government aid, the bureaucratic indifference, the denigration they have experienced, the futility and frustration they meet when they attempt to get assistance from government programs discourages them and creates a cynical attitude toward the possibility of receiving aid from a government program.

The ineffectiveness of existing programs, however, is not entirely attributable to victims' attitudes alone. The various forms of bureaucratic rationing such as lack of public information, prolonged and tedious application procedures, and numerous restrictions on eligibility contribute to the low award figures cited above.

I believe that despite its bad record, crime victims' compensation programs can be effective means of assisting victims of violent crime to be whole again. What is necessary is to eliminate those characteristics of present programs that discourage victims from making application and that prevent victims from receiving the aid they so rightly deserve.

The following section discusses the various issues and proposes certain changes in existing compensation laws. It suggests what a model bill would contain to maximize its effectiveness as a means of making victims of violent crime whole again.

Crime Victims' Compensation Laws

RATIONALE

The preamble to a crime victims' compensation bill usually states the legislative rationale for victim compensation enactment. The New York statute considers victim compensation a "matter of grace," suggesting the program has a welfare rationale. The Maryland bill rests on the concept of an absolute duty to protect its citizens, asserting a "moral responsibility" to compensate for the failure to protect the citizen. The preamble to the Hawaiian statute is simple and direct but avoids any philosophic or social rationale.

The Washington state crime victims' statute does not have a statement of purpose. However, when it was enacted, Governor Daniel Evans wrote:[17] "Any society has a duty to protect its citizens. When its protection fails, it must compensate and assist those citizens who become innocent victims of crimes."

The statement of purpose in the Alaska crime victims' compensation law is brief and gives few clues as to the rationale of the program. As in the Hawaiian preamble, it only discusses the purpose of victim compensation. It reads:

> It is the purpose of this [statute] to facilitate and permit the payment of compensation to innocent persons injured, to dependents of persons who by virtue of their relationship to the victim of a crime incur actual and reasonable expense as a result of certain serious crimes or in attempts to prevent the commission of crime or to apprehend a suspected criminal.[18]

Unlike the Alaska preamble, the statement of purpose preceding the Kentucky statute clearly indicates the rationale of the law. It is to benefit "those needy victims who are innocent victims of criminal action."[19] Kentucky is more explicit than other states about its welfare orientation, and the program is obviously based on a welfare rationale.

A model bill to compensate victims of violent crime would base itself upon the right of a victim to be made whole again *as a matter of social justice.* It would emphasize that social justice demands that the purpose of the compensation program is to provide the means by which victims of violent crime may realize that right. It would not base itself on the philosophy of assisting victims as "a matter of grace."

ELIGIBILITY

A victim may be eligible for compensation in one state while in another, exactly the same circumstances may not be considered compensable. Such discrepancies are unfair and result in post-crime victimization by the crime victims' compensation laws themselves.

Basing themselves on the orientation that victims' compensation is a form of welfare—not the victim's right—many states make awards conditional upon the victim suffering serious financial hardship. The idea that every criminally victimized citizen has the right to be made whole again is almost totally absent in state victims' compensation laws.

Because of their welfare orientation many states have adopted a "needs test" as one criterion of eligibility. In New York and Maryland no award can be granted unless there are serious financial hardships suffered as a result of the crime. The New York State Crime Victims Compensation Board writes:[20] "Where the claimant has no assets there is no problem, nor is there any problem presented when the claimant has a large amount of money together with a correspondingly good income. The difficulty arises particularly with the middle income group." One can judge from this that the merits of a needs test are debatable. There is the continual question of where the line between eligible and ineligible should be drawn. Some observers argue that the investigative costs of determining financial need are greater than the cost of additional awards that would be granted if the needs test were eliminated. Eliminating the needs test might result in only a few additional awards. Added to this argument is the nagging possibility that the determination may not be consistent or fair, because the judgment must rely on subjective criteria.

The New York State Crime Victims Compensation Board[21] realized the possible inequities inherent in a needs test and interpret the clause "serious financial hardship" somewhat liberally. In determining the claimant's assets, and thereby his eligibility, the New York board excluded from consideration: (1) the claimant's homestead; (2) the claimant's clothing and personal effects; (3) the claimant's household furniture; (4) the tools and equipment necessary for the claimant's trade or occupation; (5) life insurance on the victim in the face amount of $1,000; and (6) savings in the amount equal to one year of the claimant's income. The last two items were added in 1971 so that the victim's frugality or foresight would not exclude him from an award.

Both Kentucky and Virginia have needs tests. In the preamble to the Kentucky law this sentence appears: "Victims [of crime] may suffer serious financial hardship and state aid is a matter of grace."[22] Kentucky has printed on top of the Crime Victims

Compensation form the following: "Notice to Needy Residents of Kentucky." Explanation of the program follows. The form requires the claimant to authorize the state to investigate the claimant's financial status. The Virginia compensation program is available only to victims who suffer undue financial hardship and are unable to maintain [their] customary standard of living.

Hawaii does not have a needs requirement and offers compensation to victims regardless of economic status. This policy seems to stem from both rationales: Either the state has an "absolute duty" to protect the individual, or the state offers social insurance to the victim.

Neither Alaska, Michigan nor Washington have a needs test to determine eligibility. The victim does not have to be in serious financial hardship in order to qualify. Calvin Winslow,[23] the administrator of Washington's program, clarifies his state's position: "I feel it is cheaper for us to pay benefits to the few rich people who apply than to expend administrative funds to determine the financial status of each and every applicant."

From a practical as well as a philosophical viewpoint, needs tests are questionable. They add additional administrative and investigative costs, and these costs can outweigh the savings in the reduced number of awards.

A needs test is a form of discrimination against victims of violent crime. It implies a reluctant beneficence to the poor rather than the right to be made whole again. It discriminates against the middle class. While it is true that a majority of victims of violent crime come from the low economic groups, large numbers of middle-class citizens are victims of violent crime who should have the same rights as those in the low-income group. A needs test discriminates against them and eliminates them from eligibility for assistance. Once the principle that *every* victim of a violent crime has a right to be made whole again is accepted, the needs test becomes unnecessary.

In addition to its discriminatory nature, the needs test is also a way of injecting into the compensation program a welfare philosophy with all its concomitant denigrating and debasing implications. A needs test eliminates otherwise deserving claimants.

An example of how the welfare philosophy and the needs test discriminate against the victim is illustrated by the following quote from a report of the New York State Crime Victims Compensation Board.[24] In discussing the reason for claims being disallowed, the board reports that

> The explanation emanating from the largest number of cases is that the claimant refuses to give confidential information to the board in answering requests for copies of tax returns and asset information as an invasion of their privacy. How many of these claimants would be refused an award because of no serious financial hardship if they came forward with the necessary information cannot be estimated.

Another reason that some claims are disallowed is that institutions such as hospitals and service organizations might prepare the original claim form. In many of these cases, wrong addresses, misspelled names, and so on, are responsible for the board's inability to communicate further with the claimant. This is a very good illustration of how the welfare philosophy permeates the thinking of the staff of compensation programs and constitutes a self-justification for refusing claims and discriminating against many victims.

MINIMUM LOSS

At present, Maryland, Kentucky, and Virginia have a minimum out-of-pocket loss requirement. Recently, New York State eliminated its minimum out-of-pocket loss of $100 in medical bills or two weeks of lost earnings because it found that it eliminated from eligibility claims arising from the crime of rape and child molestation.[25] Prior to 1977 this requirement accounted for about 17 percent of all denials in New York. I suppose the rationale behind the minimum out-of-pocket loss requirement is to eliminate small and insignificant claims requiring extensive and expensive processing that would increase the cost of the program while providing very little compensation to the victim. However, a minimum loss requirement discriminates against victims of crimes such as rape and child molestation that may involve considerable physical and emotional damage to victims. If the problem of small claims' processing is important, it should be possible to set up a small claims' application and review process that could expedite the process and eliminate the costly bureaucratic review process that is applied to large claims. I suggest that the programs could set up a reduced application process and a rapid review for cases with claims of less than $100. Under these conditions, a model compensation program could eliminate the minimum out-of-pocket loss requirement.

FAMILIAL EXCLUSION

Both New York and Maryland deny awards to a member of the criminal's family or a person living in the household of the criminal. A family member is defined as a person related to the criminal within the third degree of blood relationship, or maintaining a sexual relationship with the criminal.

The Alaska, Virginia, Kentucky, and Michigan statutes provide that no compensation may be awarded if the victim is: (1) at the time of the personal injury or death, living with the offender as a member of his family or household, or maintaining a sexual relationship with the offender; or (2) a relative of the offender. The Alaska law defines a relative as a spouse, parent, grandparent, step-parent, natural-born child, adopted child, brother, half brother, sister, half sister, or spouse's parents.[26]

Michigan's law does allow victims' out-of-pocket medical expenses to be paid directly to a health-care provider if the victim resides with the criminal. The Washington state program does not have a family exclusion.

Approximately one-fourth of all homicides are committed by relatives of the victim.[27] While the frequency of victim-criminal relationship is not as great in other violent crimes, it is still significant.

If one parent of a child assaults the other parent, the victim would be ineligible for aid. In this case, even if the parents are divorced, the child would not qualify for crime victims' compensation. Similarly, an assault upon a spouse by his or her estranged mate disqualifies the victim.

A familial exclusion clause seems to have been very popular with the legislators who designed existing compensation programs. To many legislators it must have seemed plausible that members of a family would commit crimes against each other for the purpose of securing compensation from the state. The familial exclusion clause eliminates a large percentage of victims of murder and assault by members of their family. Evidently legislators believe that many victims would conspire with the offender in order to secure compensation. I suppose an infinitesmally small number of people might actually do this. However, I cannot believe that it would be difficult for investigators to ascertain if such were the case. For a claim to be eligible, there must be some injury—we're talking about victims of violent crime. It seems unlikely that a meaningful number of people would allow themselves to be physically injured just to be eligible for a claim for compensation. It is hard to see how, after the doctor bills are paid and the time lost from work compensated, there would be financial advantage to any person sufficient enough to motivate him to participate in this type of fraudulent claim. Familial exclusion is primarily a means of rationing the funds of the compensation program, for it eliminates a considerable number of victims who otherwise might be eligible for compensation.

These three restrictions on eligibility (needs test, minimum loss, familial exclusion) constitute the primary strategy of the bureaucracies administering these programs to ration compensation to victims of violent crime. The inclusion of these restrictions varies from state to state, but almost all states have one or more of them. Our model compensation program would eliminate them completely. They are discriminatory, they discourage victims from applying, and they violate the spirit of equity and social justice that should permeate the administration of the program.

The Rodino bill, which would compensate state victim programs for up to 50 percent of their cost, could exert effective pressure on the various state legislators to modify their programs by simply insisting in the bill that states having needs tests, minimal loss requirements, and familial exclusions are ineligible for federal compensation.

PUBLIC AWARENESS

One of the more subtle forms of bureaucratic rationing is to keep the public uninformed about the benefits available. The public seldom knows about victims' compensation programs because they are not publicized.

Community responses to victims' compensation programs depend upon the public's awareness of the program's existence and provisions. Lack of such public knowledge defeats the purpose of victim compensation. Of course, public awareness affects program costs in two ways: It costs money to make the public aware of the program, and the more victims who know about a program of crime victims' compensation, the more will file. Some legislators discourage publicity to keep the program budget low. Most program administrators want the public to know of the programs and what they offer in the way of benefits, but they are hampered by lack of budget for public information.

In the Maryland board's 1977 appropriations of $4,645,230, less than one-tenth of 1 percent ($4,260) was allocated for "communications." Most of this appropriation was spent on the preparation of public service announcements and distributing informational brochures.

The Washington Board has developed a brochure in both English and Spanish to explain and publicize victim compensation in that state. All daily and weekly newspapers in Washington have published one or more articles on the program.

The Washington efforts to increase public awareness, though

commendable, do not compare to the efforts made in Alaska. The Alaska board has instituted a policy of contacting victims. The office screens daily newspapers to find reports of criminal incidents and employees then attempts to contact the victim and inform him of the program. This personal approach may be more feasible in states with relatively small populations, but this argument doesn't hold for Alaska with a widely dispersed population.

Alaska requires law enforcement officers to inform victims of the existence of the program through a "Miranda-type" notice for victims. Explanatory cards ("mini-brochures") telling people about the program and directing them to "help" centers have been distributed to many attorneys and doctors for placement in their waiting rooms.

Virginia and Michigan have each made limited attempts at increasing public awareness. Both states encourage, but do not require, law enforcement officials to inform crime victims that the program exists. In Michigan, where the program went into effect in October 1977, the media publicized the program when the governor presented the first victim award. Virginia has sent explanatory pamphlets to attorneys, colleges, hospitals, and other sources of public contact.

In other states, the crime victims' compensation program is a well-kept secret. In New York State, for example, prior to the revision of the crime victims' compensation legislation, few, if any, victims of violent crime ever heard of or knew about crime victims' compensation. However, the revised legislation in New York, which became effective on January 1, 1977, was a great step forward in informing the public about compensation programs. It mandated that every police station, precinct house, or other appropriate location in New York state where a crime may be reported have on hand application forms and information brochures relating to the availability of compensation. For the first time, victims in New York are now assured that they will be told of their rights. This dramatic change in the law means that the work of the Crime Victims Compensation Board will become much more noticeable as law enforcement officials all over the state acquaint innocent victims of their rights. Just as the Miranda notice to an alleged perpetrator of a crime is required by law, now victims will be given as a matter of course a briefing on their rights and benefits under the crime victims' compensation law. The New York state law serves as a model in this respect, and I would recommend that every state modify its legislation to include informing victims of their rights under the law.

In order to facilitate public information on crime victims' compensation programs, I am including a list of all the states that have such compensation programs, their eligibility requirements, their forms of compensation, and their restrictions. Addresses victims may write to get further information are included.

APPLICATION PROCEDURES

Application procedures for awards are very similar in most states. Upon inquiry to the board or commission, claim forms are sent to the claimant. When the completed forms, including a financial resources affidavit, are returned, the executive director (or executive secretary) screens the claim to determine if the claimant meets the basic eligibility requirements. If the victim is eligible, the board informs him or her in writing that the claim is being taken under further consideration. A file is then opened and the claim is assigned to an investigator. Upon completion of the investigation, the results are given—in the states of New York, Michigan, Kentucky, Maryland, and Alaska—to a single member of the board for consideration. That member may or may not call for a hearing before making a decision on the merit of the claim. In most states if the victim is dissastisfied with the decision, he can appeal and be granted a hearing before the entire board.

In Hawaii, the victim must make application to the Hawaiian commission within eighteen months of the criminal incident. Be-

States With Crime Victims Compensation Programs[28]

	Compensation to Victims			Compensation to Survivors			Limitations			Where to Write
	Medical Expenses	Lost Earnings	Lost Property	Burial Expenses	Pension	Lump Sum	Must Be State Resident	Overall Benefits Not to Exceed	Time Limit to File Claim	
Alaska	yes	yes	no	yes	no	yes	no	$25,000 (medical) $40,000 (lost earnings)	2 years	Violent Crimes Compensation Board Pouch HO 2A Juneau, Alaska 99811
California	yes	yes	no	yes	no	yes	yes	$23,000	1 year	Victims of Crime State Board of Control 926 J Street, #300 Sacramento, Calif. 95814
Delaware	yes	yes	no	yes	yes	yes	no	$10,000	1 year	Violent Crimes Compensation Board 800 Delaware Ave., #601 Wilmington, Del. 19801
Hawaii	yes	yes	no	yes	no	yes	no	$10,000	18 mos.	Criminal Injuries Compensation P.O. Box 339 Honolulu, Hawaii 96809

State							Maximum Award	Time Limit	Agency / Address
Illinois	yes	yes	no	yes	no	no	no	$10,000	2 years (6 mos. intent)	Crime Victims Compensation 188 W. Randolph St. Chicago, Ill. 60601
Kentucky	yes	yes	no	yes	yes	no	yes	$15,000	90 days (can be extended to one year)	Crime Victims Compensation Board 113 E. Third St. Frankfort, Ky. 40601
Maryland	yes	yes	no	yes	yes	yes	no	$45,000	2 years	Criminal Injuries Compensation Board 1123 N. Eutaw St., #601 Baltimore, Md. 21201
Massachusetts	yes	yes	no	yes	no	yes	no	$10,000	1 year	Compensation to Victims of Violent Crimes (District Court where claimant resides)
Michigan	yes	yes	no	yes	yes	yes	no	$15,000	30 days (extended to 1 year for cause)	Crime Victims Compensation Board c/o Dept. of Management & Budget, Cass Bldg., Lansing, Mich. 48924
Minnesota	yes	yes	no	yes	yes	yes	no	$10,000	1 year	Minnesota Crime Reparations Board 702 American Center Bldg. St. Paul, Minn. 55101
New Jersey	yes	yes	no	yes	yes	yes	no	$10,000	1 year	Violent Crimes Compensation Board 222 West State St., Suite 201 Trenton, N.J. 08625

States With Crime Victims Compensation Programs (Continued)

	Compensation to Victims			Compensation to Survivors			Limitations			Where to Write
	Medical Expenses	Lost Earnings	Lost Property	Burial Expenses	Pension	Lump Sum	Must Be State Resident	Overall Benefits Not to Exceed	Time Limit to File Claim	
New York	yes	yes	no	yes	no	yes	no	no limit	2 years	Crime Victims Compensation Board 875 Central Ave. Albany, N.Y. 12206
North Dakota	yes	yes	no	yes	no	no	no	$25,000	1 year	Crime Victims Reparations Highway 83 North, Russel Bldg. Bismarck, N.D. 58501
Ohio	yes	yes	no	yes	when justified	when justified	no	$50,000	1 year	Victims of Crime Division Court of Claims of Ohio 30 E. Broad St., 10th floor Columbus, Ohio 43215
Pennsylvania	yes	yes	no	yes	yes	yes	yes	$25,000	1 year	Crime Victims Compensation Board Dept. of Justice Harrisburg, Pa. 17120

State							Agency
Tennessee	yes	yes	no	no	yes	$10,000	not yet determined	Criminal Injuries Compensation Fund State Board of Claims 450 James Robertson Pkwy. Nashville, Tenn. 37219
Virginia	yes	no	no	when justified	yes	$10,000	6 mos. (can be extended to 2 years)	Criminal Injuries Compensation Fund, Industrial Commission of Virginia, P.O. Box 1794 Richmond, Va. 23214
Washington	yes	yes	no	yes	yes	no limit	6 mos.	Crime Victims Compensation Division Dept. of Labor & Industries Olympia, Wash. 98504
Wisconsin	yes	yes	no	yes	no	$10,000	2 years	Crime Victims Compensation P.O. Box 7951 Madison, Wis. 53707

Note: Reprinted by permission from the New York State Crime Victims Compensation Board, *1976–1977 A Review of the Tenth Year of Operation*, p. 8.

cause the Hawaiian commission has no investigative staff, the executive secretary must do the investigative work himself. He depends heavily on police reports and hospital records. The Ninth Annual Report of the commission indicates that as a result of the investigation conducted by the executive secretary, the state was able to save $159,017.54 in awards in 1976 by eliminating claims when there was provocation, complicity, or for a noncompensable crime. The report notes the salary of a full-time investigator would be offset by the savings in awards from investigation. The quality of the investigation and the entire work of the commission would benefit from an investigative staff.

If the preliminary investigation conducted by the Hawaiian executive secretary indicates that the applicant might be eligible for an award, the case is assigned to one of the commissioners. The commissioner is responsible for presenting and summarizing the case at a formal hearing. Unlike the other states' programs, the Hawaiian program requires a formal hearing before the entire commission. A single commissioner does not have the authority to grant an award. The formal hearing requirement lengthens the time for a claim to be heard and settled. The law requires a quorum of two commissioners to convene a hearing. These administrative provisions slow down the process.

The application process in Virginia is somewhat similar to that in Hawaii. The victim contacts the Industrial Commission by letter or by completing a short form. This claim must be filed within six months of the date of injury. Upon receipt of the claim form or phone call, the Division of Crime Victim Compensation contacts the victim by mail or by phone to get a more detailed report. This detailed report is put together by a division employee with the help of the victim. The victim is not faced with a complicated form to complete without help, which might have deterred him from filing the claim. The detailed statement is mailed to the victim for him to sign and swear to its accuracy. The Compensation Division may hold a local hearing. The victim is advised of the decision by mail and, if not satisfied, can appeal to the entire Industrial Commission. If the victim is still not satisfied, he can further appeal to the Virginia State Supreme Court.

In Washington state, the victim (or survivor) must file a claim with the Crime Victims Compensation Division of the Department of Labor and Industry. The division has sixteen service locations throughout the state where assistance can be obtained in completing the necessary forms. Upon completion of the investigation, an administrative determination of the claim is made.

Much of the information required in most states is unnecessary. Nothing discourages victims from applying more than long, cumbersome, and difficult-to-complete application forms. This is particularly true of victims for whom English is a second language.

The New York CVCB, for example, required a number of sworn affidavits to verify statements made by the claimant in the application. These imposed such hardship and time-consuming effort on the part of claimants that they often gave up in disgust and did not complete the application process. Those who managed to get through the application then had to put up with long delays and incessant inquiries. The average length of time between an application and the time an award was made was seven months, during which the claimant often had to borrow money in order to bury a dead victim or to support his or her family. By the time the award was made, the claimant often owed interest as well as the original debt. New York has recently simplified its application and certainly has made an effort to speed up the process. A number of volunteers have been enlisted to help investigate claims, applications have been made available in a variety of community organizations and in hospitals, and a number of community service organizations have been mandated to screen applicants. There is no reason why there should be only a single central office for a crime victims' compensation program. Various community organizations can serve as satellite organizations that have application forms and that can assist the claimant in filling them out. Every local community service organization ought to have workers trained to handle applications from neighborhood claimants and to assist in the processing of these applications.

These procedures for speeding up and processing applications should not be left to the discretion of the program directors but should actually be written into the law.

One of the more serious problems with these compensation programs is the lack of emergency aid. I have already demonstrated that one of the most pressing needs of victims of violent crime is immediate financial assistance on an emergency basis. This is not available anywhere. If a crime victims' compensation program is to address itself to the real needs of victims, then it ought to be able to make available emergency aid. The most frequent request for emergency aid would probably be for funeral expenses or for food and shelter for a family. It should not take more than forty-eight hours to verify that a member of the family has been buried and the amount of the burial expenses. As for determining whether an emergency grant is necessary in cases of request for food and shelter, with the experience of the investigators and the staff of most crime victims' compensation boards and consultation with the staff of victim assistance programs specific criteria for determining emergencies could be developed. For example, an elderly person who is mugged and whose Social Security check has been stolen certainly is in need of immediate financial assistance. In cases where the breadwinner has been injured and out of work, a phone call to the employer can determine whether there is income available during the time he is ill. At present, where emergencies are allowed determination of the primary criterion is that the claimant be desperate; then, it still takes about two weeks for the investigation and the award to be made.

If the welfare philosophy is eliminated from the compensation program, the determination of emergency status would not be on the basis of whether the patient has money in the bank, but whether his source of income has been cut off. If that criterion were used, it would be simpler to make emergency awards on a short-term basis—let us say on a week-to-week basis—that can be checked as the application process moves forward. The emergency nature of the award could be reviewed each week. This may require a little more time and paperwork but it would be preferable to the hardships foisted on the victim by the present system.

Very often the application process is delayed because the investigator is waiting to determine whether the claimant will receive compensation from other agencies. For example, applications are often held up because of pending auto insurance claims, determination by social service agencies or by Blue Cross/Blue Shield. This whole procedure can be speeded up if the program would make the award to the applicant upon the condition that if these other agencies do make a favorable determination the compensation program be reimbursed.

OTHER ISSUES

I have mentioned the more important issues any crime victims' program must address and have described a model program that I believe would be most just.

There are a number of minor issues that, it seems to me, would improve the effectiveness of a crime victims' compensation progam. One of these is the question of whether or not claimants should be required to pay a filing fee. Some states require that the claimant pay a fee with the application. This seems socially unfair and imposes a hardship on those claimants who are in an emergency situation. The stated purpose of the filing fee is not so much a source of income but a method for eliminating inconsequential and inappropriate claims. However, I do not believe that this would eliminate such claims. What a filing fee does do is instill in the mind of the claimant a suspicion of the purposes and intentions of the compensation program. It verifies his predisposition to distrust the program, and it often acts as a deterrent to his filing the application.

Another issue is the right of the claimant to appeal the decision of the board. The New York state compensation law allows the claimant to review a final decision of the board in the courts of the state. I would recommend such a provision in any compensation program.

The following are a number of other recommendations that I would make. They are self-explanatory and do not require any lengthy justification.

1. At present the time allowed to report the crime varies from twenty-four to seventy-two hours in the several states. At least seventy-two hours should be allowed the victim to report the crime to proper authorities in order for the victim to be eligible for compensation. This requirement can be waived in extenuating circumstances such as rape and child abuse.

2. Victims should be permitted to file a claim for compensation within one year from the time of the occurrence of the crime. In special cases and for special reasons the board should be allowed to extend the time for filing to two years.

3. There should be no maximum set for an award.

4. Minor children should be eligible for award when an injury or death was caused to a member of their family. The parent of a child-victim should be eligible to receive an award.

5. The crime victims' compensation legislation should include a proposal to mandate the imposition of a specific monetary fine upon defendents convicted of certain crimes. The receipts from these penalties should be allocated to the compensation program, as well as any restitution imposed on the offender by the courts.

6. Legal fees for compensation awards are often paid out of the claimant's award. In some states, the legal fee is paid by the compensation program separate and apart from the award. It is my belief that in most cases the victim could be represented by a lay person. If there is a victim's advocate appointed by the court, he or she could represent the victim in any claim made to the

compensation program. However, in cases where the victim insists on his own attorney and wishes to be represented by a person of his own choosing, the victim should not be held responsible for the attorney's fees. These should be paid out of the budget of the compensation program. To prevent the compensation program from becoming a lucrative source of income for attorneys, I would suggest that a limit be set on the amount reimbursable to the attorney with the provision that the attorney would not be permitted to charge the claimant a fee additional to that awarded by the program.

7. One of the most frequent causes of delay is the requirement that before any award is approved, the entire commission must attend a formal hearing. This requirement is time-consuming and costly. The problem has been avoided in many states by permitting a single commission member to hold a hearing and approve an award. In some cases if the claimant wishes to challenge the decision of a single commission member, he may request a review by an additional commission member.

8. Another drawback is the procedure in Hawaii, where retroactive appropriations are made. The board makes awards but cannot be sure that it will have sufficient funds to pay them until the legislature appropriates the money. In most states this is not a problem, and it should not be in Hawaii. There is no reason for requiring appropriations by the legislature retroactively. The uncertainty of the appropriations certainly imposes on the claimant an additional concern and discourages victims from making claims.

9. Maryland, New York, Kentucky, Michigan, and Hawaii each have created a new administrative body to handle victim compensation claims. New York has a Criminal Injuries Compansation Board consisting of five members (recently enlarged from three); all must be attorneys. The board members serve seven-year terms and are appointed by the governor.

Hawaii and Alaska each have boards with three members serving three-year terms. Maryland has a three-member board which serves for five-year terms. In Maryland, at least one of the members has to have at least five years' experience as a practicing attorney. In Alaska, one member must be a physician and one an attorney. Both Maryland's and Alaska's state statutes call for the governor to designate one member as chairperson.

The Kentucky Compensation Board has five members appointed by the governor; each member is appointed for a four-year term. The Michigan board is similar to the Alaska board.

Unlike most states, Virginia and Washington did not create a new governmental agency to administer their crime victims' compensation act. Instead, Washington added a Crime Victims Compensation Division to the existing Department of Labor and Industries; and Virginia added a similar division to its Industrial Commission. However, compensation to victims of crime is different from any existing government program and, I feel, merits the establishment of a new, independent board. Tacking on administrative responsibility for victim compensation to an already existing agency has serious drawbacks. An existing agency has established rules, regulations, and practices designed to meet its original needs. These may or may not be applicable to the specific needs of administering a victims' compensation program. For the most part, they will not be. The tendency will be to use guidelines already established but inappropriate for victims. For example, some victims will undoubtedly need emergency funds immediately. Few agencies are equipped to provide such funds. In most cases two separate sets of guidelines, rules, and practices will be necessary if an agency has two separate programs to operate. Furthermore, if victims' compensation programs are placed within the purview of an existing agency, they may become a subsidiary concern—an afterthought or imposition of an additional burden—rather than the central concern of the agency.

In addition, I have serious doubts whether there would be any savings in administrative costs after the initial cost of setting up the program. It is doubtful whether any savings would be sufficient to overcome the disadvantage of saddling an existing agency with a dual purpose, a dual target population. It seems to me that a dual apparatus would develop anyway.

10. The cost to the taxpayers has been a major concern in states adopting crime victims' compensation laws. One partial solution to the cost problem would be to generate revenue by fines levied against the criminal. Such an indemnity fund was provided for in British India as early as 1837. Now most state victims' compensation programs are funded completely from annual appropriations made by the legislature. The cost of the entire program is passed on to the taxpayer.

Maryland has succeeded in easing the burden to the taxpayer by the use of an indemnity fund written into the Criminal Injuries Compensation Law. It provides that all of those convicted of criminal offenses in Maryland courts be fined $5, in addition to any other fines. These fines ($5 per conviction) are held in the Maryland indemnity fund.

The collected fines from the offenders paid for 13.6 percent of program costs of $1.7 million for 1974. In previous years, the fines collected amounted to as much as 33 percent of program costs and as little as 8 percent of those costs. There is no empirically proven answer, but experience suggests that an indemnity fund can be so designed to pay for a substantial portion of the cost of victim compensation.

The Virginia General Assembly has not made general fund appropriations to administer crime victims' compensation. Funds to pay for the program come from a fine of $10 levied against most of those convicted of committing a crime defined by the Code of Virginia. The fund has only raised $280,000 since July 1, 1976, through fiscal year 1978. Unlike the Maryland indemnity fund that merely supplements state funding, the Virginia program is entirely supported from fines collected from convicted criminals.

The Hawaiian statute uses funds available for legislative relief from within the general fund for the state's victims' compensation program. The level of funding is determined by the legislature after compensation awards have been made. In this way, the law requires legislative approval for all awards made by the Criminal Injuries Commission. The requirement delays awards and can have the effect of leaving the commission powerless. The commission can make an award, but the legislature may not appropriate sufficient funds to cover it. This system forces the victim to wait for his or her award until the legislature has approved the program's budget. The time lag, from the time the commission approves the award until the date of payment, can be from eight to twenty months. As a partial solution to this problem, the legislature in 1972 allocated $25,000 for an emergency award fund from which the commission could make awards to victims who need immediate aid. A further drawback of Hawaii's statute is that it makes no provision for protracted payments.

Both Alaska and Washington fund their crime victims' conpensation programs from general fund appropriations. The Washington statute specifically provides that the law cannot take effect until the necessary appropriations have been approved. Indirectly, then, the program must obtain legislative approval each year since failure to appropriate funds is tantamount to no program. Though this is true of most government programs, mentioning this requirement in the statute underscores the precarious postition of the program. Unfortunately, neither Washington nor Alaska has an indemnity fund.

Kentucky, like Maryland, has a system to collect from the criminals. Any compensation paid by the state creates a debt due ("owing") to the state by any person found to have committed such criminal act in either a civil or criminal court proceeding. The court may set repayment of such a debt as a condition of parole or discharge. The court may also set the schedule or amount of payments to be made. This payment schedule can be altered by the judge if the criminal's circumstances change.

Programs to compensate the victim of crime satisfy a long-standing societal need—to correct the neglect of the victim. However, most states that have enacted victim compensation have failed to fully address themselves to the problem of funding the program. The solution to the funding problem can also, in part, relate to the problem of the rehabilitation of the criminal. Retribution to the victim by the criminal can have considerable rehabilitative value even if it is used, in part, for funding compensation programs. In indemnifying the victim, the criminal will be forced to realize that his actions have not only damaged society as a whole but also a particular person.

Funding problems of victim compensation programs can be eased by such indemnity efforts on the part of the criminal with no negative effects. Since the assessment simply enters a victims' fund with awards later determined by a board or commission, there is little to motivate vengeful emotions in the criminal. The process is sufficiently impersonal, while at the same time the criminal is fully aware that he is contributing to the victim's restitution.

The possibility of an indemnity fund merits study by states considering compensation programs. Maryland has already demonstrated that an indemnity fund can be a viable method in generating revenue. Also, work-release programs and prison industry should be considered as possible sources of funds. As in Maryland, a fixed amount can be levied against the offender; or the judge in a criminal case may have an opportunity to make discretionary fines to point out that the money is for the restitution of the victim. Some of the money earned through work-release or prison industry can be paid into an indemnity fund. Restitution need not be entirely dependent on the criminal's financial status, and yet the rehabilitative value to the criminal and the victim might be realized.

11. The Law Enforcement Assistance Administration conducted a study several years ago to determine the cost of both Maryland and New York programs. In their analysis, they calculated the per-capita cost of these programs to the taxpayer. In Mary-

land, the program cost ten cents annually for each taxpayer in 1972. In New York, the per-capita program cost in 1972 was twelve cents. Nineteen percent of the New York program's total cost was for administration in 1972; today, only 17 percent of the total cost is for administration. In 1972, administrative costs in the Maryland program amounted to almost 28 percent of total costs. A more recent figure is not available at this writing.[29]

In Washington state total program costs for nearly the first three years of operation (November 1, 1973, to June 30, 1976) were $1,161,213. During that time administrative costs amounted to 17.5 percent of the total costs ($246,582). The Alaska program, in a single year of operation, exceeded Washington's three-year total. Total program costs, in fiscal year 1976 in Alaska were $1,998,993. Of this, one-third ($659,668) were administrative costs. Alaska's program costs seem high. This raises some questions about the feasibility of the compensation program personally contacting each victim.

From December 16, 1975, to December 15, 1976, the Hawaiian Criminal Injuries Commission cost the taxpayers of that state $264,554.13. About 15 percent of that ($40,707) went toward administrative costs. During this one-year period, the commission made 162 awards; on the average, each award made had an administrative cost of $251. A different indication of administrative costs, however, is the ratio of applications received to the administrative cost because each application—whether resulting in an award or not—incurs administrative costs. The commission received 174 applications in 1976 and spent $148.56 on administrative costs for every claim. The bulk of the administrative costs in Hawaii represents the salaries of the executive secretary, a secretary, office space, and office supplies.

The administrative costs for the Michigan compensation program have run 95 percent of the total cost of the program. The main reason that this figure is so high is that it includes start-up cost, since the program became effective only in October 1977. For 1977 to 1978, the Michigan state legislature has appropriated $750,000 (90.5 percent) for awards and $79,000 (9.5 percent) for administrative cost. The amounts for 1978 to 1979 are $1,500,000 (92.6 percent) for awards and $120,000 (7.4 percent) for administration. In short, the legislature expects the administrative costs to fall to a very small percentage of total program costs now that the administration has been set up.

Program costs in Virginia amount to $280,000 for the period beginning July 1, 1976, and running through fiscal year 1978. None of this money is appropriated from the general fund but is obtained exclusively from an indemnity fund. The staff consists only of the director and one secretary. The director has declined to indicate the percentage of total costs expended on administration. The small amount of money for awards and the small staff indicate a limited program but this is difficult to determine without further information.

12. Wilfred S. Pang,[30] Executive Secretary of the Hawaiian Criminal Injuries Compensation Commission, was asked his opinion concerning fraudulent claims. He replied: "Fraud can easily be detected once we examine the police report, medical reports, and scrutinize bills presented by doctors, hospitals, and others." Martin,[31] however, takes the view that

the measure of a successful fraud is that it is undiscovered, and the above statement may reflect a degree of false confidence. On the other hand, the number of fraudulent claims might actually be few. For purposes of this discussion, two types of fraudulent claims will be considered: (1) complete fraud and (2) partial fraud. A complete fraud means that the crime itself was fabricated. A partial fraud is one in which there actually has been a crime committed, but the victim misrepresents the facts in order to qualify for, or to increase the amount of, the compensation award.

A completely fabricated claim where no crime actually took place requires a degree of conspiracy difficult to achieve. The alleged victim would need to make a false report to the police. Next, the claimant would need to show injuries directly caused by the crime. A reasonable amount of corroboration might require a fellow conspirator to "witness" the crime. Last, throughout the entire fabrication, from report of the crime through investigation of it, the claim would be subjected to rather close scrutiny. It is fair to assume that the severity of the injuries that the claimant would need to suffer to warrant an appreciable award would discourage most fraudulent claimants of this type.

Partial fraud, based on an actual incident, would have a higher degree of probability and may be more difficult to expose. In this situation, a crime has actually been reported. Attendant witnesses, if any, and police reports are available. The motive for the partial fraud could be either to meet the minimum loss requirements of the victim, or to meet the financial needs requirement. The victim might try to hide his assets in order that he could appear to have the requisite financial stress for the award. However, this would be difficult if the investigation were to include a copy of his past year's income tax reports. Also, a claimant might try to inflate a claim in order to cross the threshold minimum requirement. (There is no minimum in Hawaii and Washington, so this is no problem in those states.) For example, the victim's loss of earnings might fall short of the minimum required loss. The victim might be tempted to take an extra day off of work to "recuperate" in order to inflate his loss of earnings claim above the minimum loss. Fraudulent claims based on medical expenses are less likely, but possible. The treatment of injuries requires extensive medical records and often is accompanied by an itemized invoice. It is not impossible, however, for an unscrupulous hospital employee to secure blank billing invoices and assist in this type of fraud. Even if partial frauds are successful, though, they would add little to what are already very modest awards. The risk of fraud should not be of primary concern in considering the adoption of victim compensation programs.

13. The New York and Washington programs are the only ones with no limit to the amount of compensation a victim can collect. However, before a 1976 amendment, New York did have a ceiling of $15,000 for everything except medical expenses. Maryland has a $45,000 ceiling; Michigan and Kentucky have a maximum of $15,000; and in Hawaii and Virginia the maximum is $10,000. Even if the awards are granted for an extended period of time, they cannot exceed that maximum in the aggregate.

In a letter to U.S. Congressman William J. Hughes, Calvin Winslow, administrator of the Washington Crime Victim Compensation Division, stated in regard to the maximum ceiling: "It seems to me that an innocent victim whose injuries are so severe that long-term disability occurs should not be chopped off benefits [sic] after two, three, or more years because of an artificial upper limit." [32]

Initially, the Alaska law established a maximum award of $10,000. However, the Alaska legislature has since changed this to provide an upper limit of $25,000 per victim per victimization for medical expenses and $45,000 for lost earnings.

The Hawaiian program makes awards for medical expenses, loss of earnings, pecuniary loss to dependents of deceased victims, funeral expenses, and "pain and suffering." Awards for pain and suffering are unique to Hawaii. The Criminal Injuries Commission allocated $91,229.63 during 1976 to awards on the basis of pain and suffering. Hawaii has offered compensation to crime victims since 1968, and provides the most comprehensive victim compensation of any of the American states. The program gives awards irrespective of the victim's financial position and includes pain and suffering in consideration of those awards. I believe that "pain and suffering" if included in victims compensation would make a mockery of the concept of being made whole again. The concept of making the victim whole again means that the victim be restored as nearly as is possible to his precrime physical functioning and living conditions. It is not meant to be a way for a victim to make a profit out of his victimization.

14. Two legislative approaches are used in determining which crimes are compensable—some laws provide a generic definition, others formulate a specific list of crimes to be compensated. New York, Maryland, Washington, Alaska, and Kentucky offer a generic definition. Hawaii developed a list of fifteen compensable crimes.

The Maryland and New York laws define a compensable crime as any act acknowledged as criminal by the penal code that results in personal injury to the victim. Washington and Alaska refer to criminal acts as compensable. Kentucky gives compensation for any criminally injurious act. Hawaii's legislators probably thought a limited list of compensable crimes would offer the advantage of cost control. But even this list includes almost all injuries resulting from violent crime. And this approach could lead to inequities by arbitrarily disallowing an otherwise meritorious claim.

Hawaii's "Good Samaritan" provision is a notable exception to those in other states—it allows compensation for property damage. If in preventing a crime or assisting in the apprehension of a criminal, a person suffers property loss, he or she is entitled to compensation for it. If a "Good Samaritan" ruins a suit of clothes while assisting a police officer in performance of law enforcement duties, he is compensated for the value of the clothing. I believe the simplest and most equitable policy is to declare as a compensable crime any violent crime, as defined by the Uniform Crime Reports of the FBI.

Finally, I want to stress the importance of legislation mandating crime victims' compensation programs to contract for services for the victim. Compensation programs should not be simply reimbursement mechanisms, reacting to costs incurred by the victim. They should have a proactive capacity or be able to arrange for necessary services for the victim. The New York law permits the board to contract directly for psychological counseling services for claimants who are in need of such services. The board should be sanctioned by law to adopt proactive measures to assist victims.

Legislation itself and the nature of that legislation is not necessarily a guarantee that the application and the processing of the application will be simple and speedy. It is in the nature of bureaucracies that their processes are slow and often too complicated. Administrators of these programs will need to make every effort to find the bottlenecks in the organization and to devise procedures to make the process as simple and as convenient as possible for the victim. Of course, the most effective way of insuring that administrators are making every effort to simplify and expedite the awards is accountability to the public. Accountability and public awareness are important instruments for expediting the functions of a government-assistance program.

Thinking that a model program could be designed that will automatically function effectively to help victims of violent crime is naive. No matter what the nature of the program, none will function effectively unless there is constant and considerable monitoring and demand for accountability. Administrators of programs must answer to the public for the effectiveness or lack of effectiveness of their programs. Accountability, therefore, is an extremely important issue in determining whether or not any compensation program would be effective. The next chapter discusses the various ways that accountability of such programs can be developed.

CHAPTER 7

VICTIM
ADVOCACY

How are victims to be protected from post-crime victimization by the criminal justice and human services systems? I have suggested urgently needed changes in the policies, procedures, and practices of both these systems. These changes will not occur without an increase in public awareness and organized activity directed at investigating, reporting, and documenting the changes that need to be made. The task is to mobilize public opinion and energies to pressure for changes designed ultimately to increase responsiveness to a greater number of victims. Changing the criminal justice and social welfare systems to make them more responsive to the needs of all victims requires a model different from one designed to render service to individual victims. Both models are necessary; one without the other would result only in halfway measures or in the problem being attacked episodically, with each case becoming a crisis. What is necessary is to identify the problems of victims, to address the appropriate system changes that have to be made to help victims more effectively. At the same time, one must realize that on a day-to-day basis, one cannot ignore the needs of individual victims.

Actually, advocacy has three important functions. One is to

identify the institutional and policy changes needed to insure the rights of victims. The second function is to monitor existing services, and the third to act as advocates to individual victims and their families. All of these functions are legitimate, necessary ones, but it is questionable whether these three can coexist effectively within one structure.

The dilemma is that while direct assistance to individual victims is a relatively apolitical activity, working for institutional and policy changes is historically and functionally related to the political lobbying tradition. Individual advocacy is a role played by nonpartisan, prestigious individuals or groups to protect the citizens against the institutions that already exist. They are not mandated to work for fundamental restructuring of those institutions and lack power to initiate new structures. What might be effective in getting services for one victim, for instance, might not be appropriate to the political task where highlighting and not masking the failures of an agency might be the best way to mobilize public opinion and energies to pressure for ultimately greater responsiveness to victims.[1]

The real question is whether two masters can be served simultaneously, the one committed to broad system change, and the other to individual assistance. The danger is that the concept of advocacy as a lever for social policy re-orientation will become subordinate to the immediate felt need for service to victims.[2]

What is required, therefore, is the development of two semi-independent strategies: a *social* advocacy strategy designed to bring about *system* change and an *individual* advocacy strategy designed to help *individual* victims.

Social Advocacy

A social advocacy organization would act as spokesman for victims. It would focus on the problems of crime victims as a group. Rather than looking at one case at a time, it would place its emphasis on the kind of system and policy changes necessary in the criminal justice and social welfare organizations. It would look at the whole problem of aid to victims including preventive, protective, legal, and social services. It would conduct investigations, promote legislative action, and organize public support for system changes necessary to increase the range of services available to victims.

Every crime-ridden municipality should have a Victims Advocacy Center (VAC). These should be private, nonprofit or quasi-public organizations. The VAC would have a board of directors composed of prominent citizens and community leaders interested in providing the public with information regarding the plight of victims, the state of existing resources to assist them, the role of the criminal justice and social welfare system with regard to victims, the changes in legislation and institutional practices necessary, and other important details that would result in an informed administrative, legislative, and public constituency and mobilize such a constituency to effect the necessary changes. The members of the board would be drawn from the judiciary, the social welfare system, the police and district attorney's office, the legislature and other relevant systems as well as from charitable and philanthropic organizations.

Such a center would implement these activities by conducting training programs for existing personnel in the social welfare and criminal justice systems designated as victim counselors. It would also provide such training to designated personnel in private or semiprivate organizations such as the Bar Association, community organizations, and private medical facilities.

It would also act as an information center, operating a "hot line" to inform victims about social, legal, and other available services. And it would provide consultation on preventive programs to community groups, tenants associations, senior citizens clubs, and so on.

The major activity of the VAC would be the organization of a number of task forces for the purpose of making policy studies, gathering information, and analyzing and recommending action on specific problems related to assisting victims. For example, a task force on elderly victims would focus on the many and varied problems of the aged for which there seems to be no help presently available. Of all the subgroups of victims, the greatest number of service gaps exist for the aged. This task force can address itself to some of the following issues.

- Law enforcement officials are incapable of providing adequate protection to victims who have been threatened; many older citizens are aware of this and either do not report crimes or never press charges.

- Affordable and adequate legal service is another necessity that the elderly poor lack, while legal-aid programs are always available to needy offenders.

- People living on fixed incomes suffer serious loss at the theft of even a small amount of money; and the procedures for recovering or being reimbursed for stolen Social Security funds are cumbersome and inadequate to meet the crisis that results from theft.

One very necessary function of a Victims Advocacy Center would be the organization of citizens' court-watching activities.

In the last decade, organized groups of citizens in California, Connecticut, Ohio, Missouri, Massachusetts, Illinois, New York, and many other states . . . have been recruiting and training citizens to serve as unofficial court monitors, observing court proceedings and identifying problems from a consumer's perspective.[3]

The trouble is that most of these court-watching projects are for the purpose of protecting *offender* rights. Few if any are oriented toward observing and identifying the problems of victims. A recent Law Enforcement Assistance Administration (LEAA) publication on citizens' court watching describes several such projects that it funded.[4] Three types of court-watching projects are listed: Defender Protector Projects, Law and Order Projects, and Specific Data Projects. Conspicuously missing is any mention of Victim Protector Projects. Of the eight projects described in the publication, *not a single one is victim-oriented.*

THE INVISIBLE VICTIM

Here is an example of a victim-oriented court-monitoring project—not supported by LEAA.

NEWS ITEM[5]

Crimes Against Elderly Bring Aged and Youth Into Court as Monitors

By Fred Ferretti

Inside the yellow-painted storefront on Olmstead Avenue in the East Bronx the old people were talking with the young people.

Veronica Donahue, 78 years old, her white hair covered with a hat that looked like a shower of white petals, sat on a sofa, rested her hands on her cane and said softly: "If we don't try to help one another, then what are we around for?"

And Michael Stern, 16, pudgy-cheeked and bouncy, fidgeted in a folding chair and said: "It's a shame old people get beat up. They could be my grandparents. It makes me feel bad inside."

Recurring Fear of Streets

The old people spoke of a recurring fear of the streets, and the young people of their efforts to change the widespread feeling that they were urban predators.

The old people nodded and the young people grinned. They grabbed one anothers' hands and told each other why they had all joined the court-monitoring program of the East Bronx Council on the Aging, then they climbed into a caravan of cars for the 15-minute ride to the County Courthouse, where they were to watch a man be sentenced for stealing checks from a 78-year-old man.

The monitoring program, an outgrowth of a pilot project called Helping Aged Needing Direction (HAND), begun earlier this year in the Bronx, has recruited not only a corps of elderly people, but also has recently enlisted a group of youngsters under a grant from the New York City Youth Board.

The volunteers in the program, called An Attack on Crime Against the Elderly, attend court sessions, learn the steps from arrest or indictment through conviction or acquittal, assist old people who are victims of street crimes and, perhaps most important, establish themselves as an open-intimidating presence in court while those accused of crimes against the aged pass through the procedures of the criminal-justice system.

180

Victim Advocacy

The program, directed by a lawyer, Stephen Haney, and a social worker, Judy Haufman, is financed by the Greater New York Fund, Citibank, Chemical Bank and private donors, in addition to the Youth Board.

The program has a budget of $75,000 for this year.

The volunteers, after receiving reports on elderly victims of street crimes from the 43rd Precinct, contact the victims by phone and in person, help them to reach the various city agencies they might have to deal with, and give them the support they need to go through the often time-consuming and frustrating series of court appearances they have to, according to Mr. Haney.

As important as overcoming a victim's reluctance to testify against an assailant is the practice of the group to send delegations of the elderly—and recently of the young—to court when it is known that a person alleged to have committed a crime against someone old is to be arraigned, tried or sentenced.

"We want ourselves felt by all the components of the criminal-justice system," Mr. Haney said. "We want not only to see how it operates, but we want to keep those in aware of the interests of the victim and the community."

Whether there has been any impact upon the conviction rate from the monitoring program has not so far become evident but some defense lawyers have insisted that it unfairly influences the legal process. When the monitoring began, two months ago, one judge noted that courtrooms were public places and said that he welcomed the expression of community interest, suggesting that more activities like them could stimulate broader social action.

The judge, Ivan Warner, presiding over a $6 mugging case in which the jaw of an 83-year-old woman was fractured, noted:

"Maybe it [the monitoring] will result in some public awareness and get something done."

Victim protector court watching can produce concrete evidence of post-crime victimization by the courts. It can pinpoint the court procedures and processes that need to be changed to insure the rights of victims, and it can make the judiciary aware that the public is concerned and observing the judicial process to insure that victims' rights are not being violated.

Funding is an important issue in the effectiveness of a social advocacy organization. If leaders of these organizations have to invest the major portion of their working time in securing funds, the organization is bound to become ineffective.

A group mandated to work for change and to develop a consumer and institutional constituency to support that change should not also have to develop its constituency to fight for survival money. To work for social change, whatever the arena, is a demanding, often frustrating process, and to have to go the same route for funding sets up unnecessary obstacles and insures increased difficulty in sustaining community support.[6]

My proposal for the funding of such victims' advocacy centers is simple. LEAA has spent millions of dollars on crime-prevention programs, on programs for the rehabilitation of the offender, on offender court-watching projects, and on police hardware. Some of the money spent by LEAA on offender programs could be diverted to grants for nonprofit organizations to set up victims' advocacy centers. These would not be expensive operations. They could utilize volunteer labor, particularly in towns where there are university students. The argument may be made that the victims' assistance programs LEAA already supports could perform this function. From my experience, however, it is quite clear that it is almost impossible for an organization that concerns itself primarily with direct service to individual victims and their needs to also serve as the kind of mobilization center for public opinion, investigation, legislative lobbying, and other activities necessary to accomplish effective social change. Therefore, these two functions should be divided. If it is impossible to divide these functions, then I would suggest victims' assistance programs funded by LEAA be required to spend at least 50 percent or more of their budget on advocate activities addressed not to the individual victim but to victims' problems within the system.

Individual Advocacy

Changes in the criminal justice and human service systems may succeed in bringing victims certain rights from which they are presently disenfranchised. But being entitled to these rights does not guarantee that the individual victim will be given them. Being eligible and entitled to certain government services does not assure victims they will receive those benefits. In the first place, victims are not likely to know exactly what they are entitled to. The difficulty lies in obtaining information about the operation of an agency. Innumerable regulations, rules, and practices, about which it is impossible for most citizens to be fully informed, govern the agency's operation. In fact, due to the large size of some agencies, often even its staff members are not fully informed of its rules. I have spent hours trying to find out whom to talk to for information about the operation of an agency. Not only did staff members not wish to give the information, which is sometimes true, but even if they did, they often did not know how or where to find it. It is not unusual to be referred from person to person without ever finding what you are looking for.

For the most part, the staff of these government services view applicants more as supplicants and rip-off artists. They see themselves as protecting the agency from freeloaders. In spite of all the public and political propaganda that these public services are rights that claimants have, the staff members see themselves as dispensing privileges. They feel the more immediate responsibility to their own administrative management rather than to the public. Even where they feel some responsibility to the public, their individual clients are not thought of as members of "the public." That public is always a broad, general, amorphous mass that is "watching" them relate to the client.

Among the staffs of government services, fearful attitudes prevail—for what may be a simple administrative error in a nongovernmental organization could very easily become not only an administrative matter but a political issue as well. Staff members therefore wish to keep their administrative operation and decisions as quiet and private as possible. The staffs of these agencies are constantly in fear of being accused of being too liberal, too conservative, too free with government money, too obstructionist with people's entitlements, and so on.

This bureaucratic state of apprehension results in a rigidity that makes rules and regulations absolutely inviolate regardless of the human condition. Since they have psychologically ruled out any personal consideration, staff members become completely mechanized, dependent on and defensive of regulations and rules. All of this adds up to what most people believe to be bureaucratic indifference.

Almost every employee in the human service and criminal justice systems will offer the desire to "help others" as one of his prime motives for choosing his work. This is a sincere and often a profound motivation. To the worker "helping others" is a humanitarian principle, a concept he considers important. He sees himself as serving those in need. His satisfaction lies in providing that service; in so doing he realizes his competence. However, this can and often does take on negative dimensions. The staff member may see the client essentially as a recipient of his special talents, and he may need the client to reinforce his self-concept as an expert or authority. The implication of patronage and the lack of reciprocity are inherent dangers, and interfere with a peer-service attitude.

There is an interesting psychological phenomenon in the relationship between a service agency and its "clients"—between the "helpers" and the "helped." When one individual helps another voluntarily, he or she does so out of some feeling of quid pro quo or compassion, perhaps even duty or guilt. Whatever the reason, there exists a mixed feeling of compassion and commitment, signifying some degree of humanity. But when helping becomes institutionalized—when helping becomes a business—personal feelings such as compassion and commitment give way to institutionalized attitudes of authority and benevolent despotism that drain the humanity out of the relationship.

The attitude of the person receiving the help also differs when it is given by a concerned individual rather than when it is institutionalized. In the first instance, the "helped" person experiences compassion, sympathy, warmth, and humanity. He does not feel demeaned, denigrated, or inferior. But in the institutionalized role of "client," he experiences powerlessness and being put down. He is forced into the role of "supplicant," and if he doesn't play properly, he will be denied the help he is seeking. These institutionalized roles are so imperative that the claimant himself often assumes the supplicant role without ever being aware of it. Institutional roles are powerful social contracts that define the conditions of a relationship for the purpose of directing and controlling people's attitudes and behavior. It is very difficult to overcome and step outside these prescribed roles. That is why it is so difficult for the institutionalized "helper" not to feel and act like a benevolent despot and the "client" not to feel and act like a supplicant.

Once you become a "client," you are considered a "supplicant" and deprived of certain consumer rights. Time becomes the exclusive property of the agency. Your time is completely at its disposal and convenience. The urgency of your need takes second place to administrative policies, procedures, and practices that are not necessarily efficient, practical, or reasonable. In fact, the time it takes to provide the service contains a large element of "indifferent time," in which forms lay on desks for weeks—even months—regardless of the case's urgency.

Information is either concealed or rationed according to the administrative needs of the agency rather than the needs of the client.

Reverse accountability is the general practice. You are accountable to them! The agency is accountable only unto itself. Demands for explanations or rationales for rules and regulations are considered impudent and improper for a supplicant.

My personal experience both as an advocate for victims and as a "client" was a surprising revelation. As an advocate I was effectively cool, deliberate, and relentless in my pursuit of information and the service to which the victim was entitled. I dealt with the staffs of service agencies with authority and I refused to be put off. I had the power of a large, recognized community group to back me up and I used it when necessary.

Recently I filed a claim with one of the government services. Whenever I tried to get specific information about their decisions regarding my case, I found myself reacting to the frustrations of dealing with bureaucratic indifference with exasperation and sometimes anger. From the municipal to the federal level government services appeared to me as Kafkaesque territory where mysterious agencies function behind opaque barriers that have sanctimonious signposts reading "come unto me all ye that are heavy laden." The discrepancy between the rhetoric of their purposes and the manner of their functioning stirred in me a deep sense of resentment of the hypocrisy and injustice so characteristic of human service agencies. Like everyone else, I hate to be a "patsy." Yet I felt I had been taken by the staff of this agency. Whether it was information, explanation, or service that I needed, I came away unsatisfied, frustrated, and angry with myself afterward when I realized that I didn't get what I sought. Staff members made me feel as if I were a beggar—as if I was asking for something they were going to be good enough to bestow on me even though I didn't deserve it. I felt powerless.

Victims who need assistance and who find themselves stymied and frustrated by the human service and criminal justice systems need individual help. That is why I am proposing a victim's advocate appointed by the court. Such an advocate will not only assist the individual victim in matters pertaining to his rights within the criminal justice system, but would also be available to the victim in his struggle against post-crime victimization by the human service system. I think it is worthwhile to summarize what I have previously said about the function of a court-appointed victim's advocate within the criminal justice system.

1. In the case of threat by the offender and the need for police protection, the advocate could advise the victim of the necessary procedure to secure a protection order. He can follow the process assuring that each step is properly carried out, keep the police informed of any attempted violation, and in the event of violation, follow through together with the district attorney in prosecution.

2. The advocate can inform the victim of the status of his case at each stage of the prosecutory process.

3. The advocate would plead the cause of the victim before the judge to prevent interminable and abusive use of postponements.

4. The advocate would represent the victim in plea bargaining.

5. If restitution becomes part of the sentencing procedure, the victim's advocate would represent the victim's interest in determining the amount and manner of restitution.

6. The advocate can certify to the satisfaction of the police and court that recovered stolen property does indeed belong to the victim and thereby speed up the process of getting property returned to the victim.

By the very act of appointing a victim's advocate with sanction to intervene with scheduling and procedures on behalf of the victim, the court provides itself with a form of quality control against post-crime victimization. The advocate makes the judicial process smoother for both victims and the court. He functions to aid both the court and the victim by providing a human link, a line of communication—facilitating the involvement of the victim. He symbolizes to the victim the court's sincere intention to provide justice.

The lower middle classes, the blue-collar workers, and other low-income persons faced with fragmented facilities, hampered by barriers of language, and embittered by the impersonal, officious, and institutionalized manner with which they are frequently met, often are overwhelmed and too often they reject or are rejected by, the only sources of aid available to them. Their problems get worse. Only at the point of crisis do they turn again for help.

The victim's advocate is a link between the victim and community resources. As such he performs the following jobs:

1. He maintains a complete roster of service agencies and organizations within his community. He knows what type of service they provide and what their rules and regulations are.

2. He establishes and maintains contact as an officer of the court with these community facilities. He gets to know the proper administrative personnel who can facilitate referrals, and he keeps up a cordial relationship with them.

3. He exercises tracer and follow-through procedures to see that the victim makes and keeps his appointments. He continually checks to see that the victim is receiving the maximum potential service of an agency with the minimum delay.

4. He receives complaints from the victim about the lack of or poor quality of service, and investigates in the victim's interest.

To summarize, he functions as an expediter of victim's claims before the compensation board, the welfare department, the hospitals, and other agencies that provide services to which the victim may be entitled.

There is already a large body of knowledge, skill, procedures, and experience that can be drawn upon to develop this new role in the criminal justice system. Two groups that have developed prototypes of this role are veteran's organizations through their service representatives and the labor movement through their union counselors. These groups saw the need for such a role when they realized that their members needed help to get the full benefits to which they were entitled from public and community service agencies. Frequently, the main reason the member failed to receive these benefits was that he did not know what help was available or how to get it. Therefore, the original function of the union counselor and the service representative was an educational one. They informed members of their privileges and assisted them by interpreting the rules, regulations, and laws. In many instances bureaucratic red tape, incompetence, or indifference kept people from receiving benefits. In these cases the service representative or union counselor often represented the member, attempting to break through the unnecessary delay, using the power of his organization as a lever if needed. Where the rules and regulations were unclear, or a person's rights to certain benefits were questioned, the representative performed the function of a lay attorney, arguing the case on behalf of the member of his organization. Union counselors and veteran's service representatives have helped millions secure the benefits and health and education services they were not able to obtain themselves.[7]

If the victim's advocate is to be the client's representative, who is to employ him, where is he based, and how can he develop sufficient "muscle" to be effective with community agencies? Sweden's ombudsman has his base in the government, and his source of power is directly political and official. The service representative is employed by the veteran's organization; his power is unofficial but lies in his affiliation with an important political interest group. The union counselor, who is usually a volunteer, has the union as his base; his source of power, too, is unofficial, but he has the backing of a local group that has ties to city, state, and national union politics. But the model that provides the advocate with the most "muscle" is the one in which his power is official.[8]

Advocacy power can take different forms. There is *legal* power that provides the advocate with resources for *enforcement* of rights of the individual. A court appointee would have the power of the court behind him. He would have the right to certain information that would be difficult for anyone else to get; he would have the right to institute investigations; and in general, he would have the same rights as any other arm of the court, such as probation officers, and so on. This power would make a victim's advocate more effective in helping the victim. Without such power, attempts on the part of the advocate to secure information, to investigate agency rules, regulations, and procedures, and to be privy to information about the agency and its relationship to the victim would be difficult. The other form of power an advocate can have is as a representative of a community organization with a constituency that has established itself in the community as powerful enough to exercise pressure on various public agencies and organizations. Not too many organizations of this kind exist; therefore, I feel that a victim's advocate appointed by the court would be far more effective in assisting individual victims than having victims depend on the presence of an organized pressure group to provide the clout.

In its 1976–1977 review of its tenth year of operation, the New York Crime Victims Compensation Board suggests that it "be empowered to become the advocate office for victims in the state; provide for multi-service techniques to assist crime victims in their recovery; allow for advocates to speak for victims in obtaining restitution from convicted felons."[9] I believe this is like asking a judge in a criminal case to be the lawyer for the victim at the same time. The function of the Crime Victims Compensation Board is to sit in judgment and make decisions regarding claims made by victims. It cannot represent the victim in that claim at the same time. This foolish proposal is nothing but a political public relations gimmick.

Advocacy is a *consumer* mechanism for accountability, not a *provider* mechanism. Providers cannot be advocates for consumers at the same time they are providers. A genuine conflict of interest exists that cannot be disguised even by well-intentioned rhetoric. An advocate is a person committed to the interests of the consumer—in the case of victims, committed to represent and fight for the interests of victims. He is not a mediator who seeks to arbitrate between the victim and the criminal justice system. He does not stand above the criminal justice system and the victim and attempt to arrive at a satisfactory compromise between them. The advocate is guided not by the rules or principles of conflict mediation but by the rules and principles of fighting for the just entitlements of the victim.

The word advocate implies more than a mediator or compromiser. It implies a total commitment to one side—the side of the victim.

To ask the organization that has a vested interest in the established system to mount the effort required to change the organization, to be more responsive to victims, is not feasible. The advocates would be in danger of becoming powerful allies, not of the victims but of the institutions. It is likely that the watered-down pressure for change that would result could easily be absorbed by the current system without any real change.[10]

The danger that court-appointed victim's advocates might themselves become bureaucratized cannot be ignored. But the very nature of their work will set them in conflict with the existing offender-oriented practices. They would constitute within the criminal justice system a countervailing force to the present monopoly of offender-oriented bureaucrats. Utilizing conflict between bureaucratic elements of a system is a well-known strategy to bring about system change. A counter force to the offender-oriented attitudes within the criminal justice system— even if a bureaucratic one—would be a great step forward.

What kind of training should be required of a victim's advocate? Need he be a lawyer or would paralegal training be sufficient? I have given careful thought to the question, and would like to see criminal justice schools create a new specialization offering an M.A. degree in Victimology. Members of the legal profession who wish to make a career in victimology would not be excluded; but at the same time this career would not be limited to members of the bar. I am convinced that the law school offender-oriented curriculum would be an impediment to the training of an advocate dedicated to the rights of victims.

The proposals for social advocacy and for a court-appointed

victim's advocate are the result of data collected, observations made, and conclusions I have reached from the experiences of the Crime Victims Service Center. They are concrete, rational, and practical. They have not just been "dreamed up" but are based on individual advocacy efforts and familiarity with social advocacy centers, including the Massachusetts Child Advocacy Center, an organization that has achieved considerable success in improving children's services.

CHAPTER 8

DISASTER AID

When implemented, I believe the proposals I have made in this book will bring relief to the 3 to 5 million citizens who each year become victims of violent crime. When the thirty or more states that have not yet done so enact crime victims' compensation laws, and, if the public is concerned enough to monitor these programs, individual victims throughout the country will have a resource for aid that will alleviate some of the agony and hardship they now experience.

But the *social* problem of victimization will not be entirely alleviated by compensation to individual victims. Compensation will not find victims new homes or apartments in ghettos where housing units have been destroyed by crime. Compensation to individual victims will not remedy the damage that crime inflicts on communities and neighborhoods. It is not enough to aid the individual victims of crime. The neighborhoods damaged by crime must be rehabilitated just as the areas damaged by a natural disaster are given federal aid to restore the community to normal functioning.

Through this book I have argued that some high-crime areas of large metropolitan cities are "disaster" areas in every sense of the word and that the victims in these areas are disaster victims no less than victims of natural disasters. Arson, vandalism, and criminal negligence on the part of landlords destroy scores of housing units, stores, and small businesses. Since nothing is done and the destruction is continuous, the effect is cumulative until entire areas of several square blocks are abandoned in ruin.

Like the ruins of Berlin and other European cities after the saturation bombing of World War II, whole areas are destroyed. The population abandons the area, and only the desperately poor, the helpless elderly, and the dehumanized vagrants, tramps, and homeless nomads remain.

All the community support systems that can help people abandon the area. Relatives, friends, churches, and community service organizations leave. Only the police remain. The buildings in these areas which once were teeming with life now resemble tombstones.

These pockets of rubble and ruin are the playground of what Bronx Police Commander Anthony Bouza has called "feral children." These are the breeding places for young criminals.

It is not sufficient to understand the tragedy of individual victims of crime; it is essential to comprehend the *social* tragedy—the tragedy of the crime-ridden city.

Agencies and criminologists find it convenient to establish "crime rates" as a measure of the social problem of crime and the effectiveness of law enforcement. But crime rates are not a true picture of the effectiveness of law enforcement agencies, nor do they illuminate the social problem. As a barometer of the social problem of criminal behavior, the crime rate is inadequate. Any analysis of the social problem of crime must take into account not only the number of crimes but the extent of the damage resulting from them. The loss to individuals and property is essential information in assessing the *social problem*. The victims of violent crime are the true indicators of the extent and depth of violent criminal behavior. Adequate information about victimization, however, is not available.

Disaster Aid

No information is available about the degree of seriousness of physical and economic harm suffered by individual victims of violent crime. The extent of harm in a particular crime is not necessarily considered in determining to what degree the law has been violated. How much community and individual damage has been done is crucial in estimating the seriousness of a crime. But I am not aware of any statistical records that estimate the social damage caused by crime.

The necessity for data on "seriousness" was suggested as early as 1969 in the staff report to the National Commission on the Causes and Preventions of Violence.[1]

The report suggests that an index of crime should accurately weight the relative seriousness of each crime and discusses using Sellin and Wolfgang's psycho-physical scaling technique,[2] which demonstrates how this can be done. Sellin and Wolfgang asked a representative sample of people to judge the relative seriousness of various crimes. The rating system that resulted from the sampling showed, for example, that those interviewed, who came from different backgrounds, "on the average thought homicide to be about two and a half times more serious than rape."[3]

To improve the scale,

... the Science and Technology Task Force of the commission interpolated the Sellin-Wolfgang scores onto an additive scale of a relative amount lost by the individual victim of a crime. The resulting ranking does not follow the same order as the UCR. The "disutility" scale suggests that aggravated assault is more serious than robbery, while the UCR ranking suggests the opposite.[4]

The groundwork has already been laid for an index that accurately reflects the seriousness of the crime it reports. Although the task force recommended that the Uniform Crime Report should give top priority to this matter almost ten years ago, Marvin Wolfgang has only recently been given funds to develop his system for the collection of criminal statistics indicating the amount of harm, suffering, loss to the community or to the victims of violent crime.

A crime-reporting system capable of providing data on the seriousness of each crime and a cumulative index of the extent of the damage or loss to individuals and communities is necessary.

Take this case, for example: An arsonist who sets fire to a single home is presently guilty of the same crime as an arsonist who sets fire to an apartment house and destroys twenty-five housing units. I believe the burning of twenty-five housing units is much more serious than the destruction of a single home. Yet the law would charge both offenders with the same crime. Each would be counted as a single crime, and the relative seriousness of each would be ignored in the present system of crime reporting. But the community or neighborhood that is faced, overnight, with the loss of twenty-five housing units has suffered a disaster, and the burned-out families are truly disaster victims.

Despite all the statistics the crime rate figures do not begin to reveal the true toll that crime takes on individuals and communities. This is not simply because the statistics are inaccurate; the main problem is that they are measuring with a rigid ruler rather than a flexible tape. How serious the damage and loss to a community and the individuals in it is cannot be measured by counting the number and classification of offenses committed. If ever there was an example of how an offender orientation blinds one to the total problem of crime and justice, it is the present method of crime reporting. It is possible—even likely—that the crime rate could go down and yet the seriousness of the damage and loss due to crime—the social loss—would increase.

I believe crime would be greatly deterred if offenders were held responsible for the seriousness of the loss and damage to a community or individual. Holding the offender socially responsible by grading the seriousness of the crime and gearing sentences to the concept of social as well as legal seriousness would replace the old value system the offender may use to evaluate the consequences if he is caught. Instead of an offender considering the relative consequences of a felony or a misdemeanor charge, he would be faced with weighing consequences of twice the severity of punishment—regardless of the legal crime category.

Why don't we keep account of crime in this way? Technology is not the problem. The psychological mind set—the offender orientation and the social and political context for it—accounts for the failure to track the seriousness of the damage crime inflicts on the communities and citizens of the nation.

At the time of the looting following the New York blackout in July 1977 President Carter refused to declare the city a disaster area because the blackout and looting was not a "natural disaster." But the Small Business Administration conferred disaster status on New York City and Westchester County.

By its actions the government acknowledged, for the first time, that disaster status is legitimate and available for some victims of crime—small businessmen who suffer loss of business property—while denying aid to individual citizens who suffered personal violence as well as loss of personal property.

Government services such as welfare, unemployment insurance, housing, and so on, have adamantly refused to provide emergency aid to victims of violent crime on the grounds that the only emergencies eligible for aid are those caused by natural disasters.

The opponents of disaster status for victims of violent crime—though they will admit to the desperate conditions of violent crime victims—have steadfastly maintained that the legislation authorizing disaster aid does not allow aid for "man-made" disasters such as crime—that is, the *law* will not allow it.

When I first developed the idea of disaster status for victims, I envisioned that a long legislative battle would be necessary to win victims this status. Yet it turns out that one man, the President, can decide what constitutes a disaster—and he is not constrained to limit aid to victims of natural disasters only.

On August 7, 1978, President Carter dealt a death blow to the argument that disaster aid is for victims of natural disasters only when for the first time he approved disaster status for victims of a man-made disaster.

NEWS ITEM[5]

Carter Approves Emergency Help for Love Canal
Carey Promises State Aid to Polluted Niagara Area

by Donald G. McNeil Jr.

President Carter approved Federal emergency financial aid last night for the Love Canal area of Niagara Falls, N.Y., where chemical leakage from an old landfill has endangered the health of residents whose backyards border the site.

The declaration allows the Federal Disaster Assistance Administration to add Federal funds and the help of Federal agencies to state and local efforts to "save lives, protect property, public health and safety, or avert the threat of a disaster." It was not immediately clear how much money the Government would make available.

And last night, Governor Carey said the state would commit state funds "on a 50-50 basis" with the Federal Government to pay for the cleanup. Speaking to a news conference in Albany before a planned visit to the Love Canal site, the Governor said the state would begin to spend its share—which he estimated at as much as $4 million—immediately . . .

Love Canal is a landmark case. Ordinarily, the residents of a chemically contaminated area would be forced to resort to civil suits to recover damages. Such a suit might take years while the residents live in constant danger of bearing children with birth defects, or of the occurrence of serious brain or nerve damage in their growing children. This is a real emergency requiring *immediate* evacuation. Thirty-seven families, for example, were offered Air Force housing. The State paid for hotel rooms, moving costs, and offered rent vouchers of $300 a month to fifteen families. This could not possibly been accomplished by a civil suit. Court action is simply not a mechanism for disaster aid, whether the disaster is natural or man-made.

Some people may claim—in defense of President Carter's action—that the Love Canal situation is a natural disaster since it involves the destruction of the "natural" environment. But the fact that the natural environment is affected by pollution or contamination of some sort is not what makes it a "natural" disaster. "Natural" disaster is not a descriptive term; it is an attributive one which pinpoints the *cause* or responsibility for disasters. The essential feature of a natural disaster is that it is caused by forces of nature over which man has no control. When lightning strikes a tree and a thousand acres of forest are burned, that is a natural disaster. But if someone carelessly throws a match and burns out a thousand acres of forest, that is a man-made disaster though it may cause the same destruction to the same natural environment.

Carter acted appropriately and his decision has far-reaching implications for victims of violent crime. First, he has established that the definition of a disaster is not a matter of law but simply an administrative decision. Second, the definition of a disaster need not be limited to natural disasters exclusively and can include man-made ones as well. Third, disaster status can be invoked to avoid impending or threatened disasters.

I propose that the mayors of New York, Detroit, Chicago, and several other crime-ridden large metropolitan cities ask the President to declare the worst neighborhoods in their cities disaster areas. It is not necessary to wait for another riot. Surely the yearly number of housing units lost, the number of stores and other commercial establishments damaged or destroyed, the number of individuals killed or injured by arson, vandalism, and violence in any one of these cities is greater than the destruction caused by most natural disasters aided by the FDAA. The rehabilitation of these areas is an immediate necessity to avoid further loss and suffering of disastrous proportions. Now is the time to test the sanctimonious police rhetoric about "crime in the streets." Not more police but the rehabilitation of the "streets" may be a more effective crime-prevention approach.

Money should be requested for restoration and to clear the

rubble and ruin that cannot be restored, to rehabilitate housing units that now lie empty and abandoned, to bring life again to neighborhoods that now stand deserted and dead. Such a rehabilitation program would also provide thousands of jobs and new hope to those victimized by society and by crime.

If the President rejects the mayors' requests, he would have to answer to the American public. If the public is made aware of the victim problem and clearly shows it cares, it would be difficult for the President to ignore the weight of such public opinion.

As previously mentioned, the technology for developing a computerized statistical accounting system of the seriousness of crime—both individual and community—has been available for years, although neither the FBI nor the Law Enforcement Assistance Administration has made any significant effort to develop such a system. It is an omission for which LEAA ought to be held accountable.

Conclusion

The purpose of this book is to bring to the attention of the public and responsible government officials and legislators the fact that America has failed to make a national commitment to the victims of violent crime. Our nation has failed to provide guarantees of victims' rights as citizens to equality before the law and their right to be made whole again as a matter of social justice.

I have illustrated how the scales of justice are out of balance, and I have highlighted the social, political, and economic issues that need to be addressed to plan for victims' aid.

The agony of victims of violent crime is an invisible disaster, hidden from public view. Nothing short of mobilization of the nation's resources for disaster aid will remedy their situation. Disaster aid, however, is not to be thought of only as financial aid.

Disaster Aid

The catastrophe of crime requires that the entire resources of the country be mobilized to assist stricken communities and individuals. In addition to financial assistance: a program must establish a declaration of the rights of victims and recommend changes in the various components of the criminal justice (courts, police, corrections, and so on) and human service systems to implement these rights; a nationwide compensation program to make victims whole again; a disaster-aid program to rehabilitate neighborhoods and communities destroyed by crime; and appointed government officers (victim's advocates) dedicated to defending the rights of victims.

Some of these programs will require new legislation and administrative decision. All will require organized political pressure by an active and knowledgeable public constituency.

Our nation's commitment to human rights is weakened by our failure to make a commitment to the rights of victims of violent crime. My final proposal, therefore, is that a national effort for a commitment to victims of violent crime be launched by the appointment of a Presidential Commission on Victims of Crime to set guidelines for changes in the criminal justice and human service systems, to recommend necessary legislation to adequately compensate victims, and to outline the procedures for training the necessary manpower to assist victims.

Without such a national effort, the invisible virus of violent crime will continue to inflict disaster on our communities and neighborhoods, and the citizens of America.

NOTES

EPIGRAPH

1. Harold Rosenberg, "The Shadow of the Furies," *New York Review of Books,* Vol. 23, nos. 21 and 22, 20 Jan. 1977, p. 49.

CHAPTER 1

1. Agatha Christie, *An Autobiography* (New York: Dodd, Mead, & Co., 1977), p. 425.
2. Emanuel Perlmutter, "Couple, Recently Robbed, Take Their Lives Citing Fear," *New York Times,* 17 Oct. 1976, p 51.
3. Judy Klemesrud, "Many Elderly in the Bronx Spend Their Lives in Terror of Crime," *New York Times,* 12 Nov. 1976, p. B6.
4. Judy Klemesrud, "Police Unit Hunts Predatory Youths, Aid their Aged, Terrorized Victims," *New York Times,* 13 Nov. 1976, p. 11.
5. Klemesrud, "Many Elderly in the Bronx Spend Their Lives in Terror," p. B6.
6. U. S. Department of Justice, Federal Bureau of Investigation, *Crime in the United States: Uniform Crime Reports–1977* (Washington, D.C.: U.S. Government Printing Office, 1978), p. 6.
7. *Ibid.*
8. The Staff report to the National Commission on the Causes and Prevention of Violence, prepared by Donald J. Mulvihill and and Melvin M. Tumin with Lynn A. Curtis, reports that three surveys were done for the Commission. The National Opinion Research Center (NORC) study indicated that the 1965 victim rate for violent Index crimes was almost double the comparable UCR rate for individuals, while the 1965 victim rate of the three Index property crimes combined was more than double the comparable UCR rate.
9. Robert D. McFadden, *New York Times,* 14 July 1977, p. A1.
10. Robert D. McFadden, *New York Times,* 15 July 1977, p. A1.
11. Federal Disaster Assistance Administration (FDAA), *U.S. Department of Housing and Urban Development, Annual Report 1976* (Washington, D.C.: U.S. Government Printing Office 1977), p. 50.
12. Ibid., p. 50.
13. Ibid., p. 50.
14. Ibid., p. 60.
15. Hermann Mannheim, *Comparative Criminology* (Boston: Houghton Mifflin Company, 1965), p. 675. Quoted in a paper by Robert A. Silverman, "Victim Precipitation: An Examination of the Concept" in *Victimology: A New Focus, Vol. 1,* ed. Israel Drapkin and Emilio Viano (Lexington, Mass.: R.C. Heath and Company, 1974), p. 99.
16. *New York Times,* 27 May 1977, p. A9.

Notes

17. H.R. 3686, 95th Congress, 1st Session, February 17, 1977. "A Bill to provide for grants to states for the payment of compensation to persons injured by certain criminal acts and omissions and for other purposes (referred to the Committee on the Judiciary).

CHAPTER 2

1. "Justice Dept. May Create New Crime-Report Agency," *New York Times,* 20 Apr. 1977, p. 19.

2. United States Department of Justice, Federal Bureau of Investigation, *Crime In the United States—1976, Uniform Crime Reports* (UCR), (Washington, D.C. Government Printing Office, 1977).

3. Ibid., p. 7.

4. Ibid., p. 12.

5. Ibid., p. 15.

6. Ibid., p. 18.

7. Marvin E. Wolfgang, "Crimes of Violence." Consultant paper to the President's Commission on Law Enforcement and Administration of Justice, *Task Force Report: Crime and Its Impact on Assessment* (Washington, D.C.: U.S. Government Printing Office, 1967) p. 32. Cited in Donald J. Mulvihill, Melvin M. Tumin, and Lynn A. Curtis, *Crimes of Violence, Vol. 2,* Staff Report to the National Commission on the Causes and Prevention of Violence December 1969, pp. 17–18.

8. Fred J. Cook, "There's Always a Crime Wave—How Bad Is This One?" *New York Times Magazine,* 6 Oct. 1968, p. 132. Cited in Mulvihill, Tumin, and Curtis, *Crimes of Violence, Vol. 2,* Staff Report to the National Commission on the Causes and Prevention of Violence, (Washington, D.C.: U.S. Government Printing Office December 1969), p. 18.

9. Mulvihill, Tumin, and Curtis, *Crimes of Violence, Vol. 2,* Staff Report to the National Commission on the Causes and Prevention of Violence (Washington, D.C.: U.S. Government Printing Office, December 1969), p. 29.

10. Report of the counselor from a case file of the Crime Victims Service Center, 1975.

11. Mulvihill, Tumin, and Curtis, *Crimes of Violence, Vol. 2,* p. 19.

12. UCR 1976, p. 11.

13. Ibid., p. 11.

14. Ibid., p. 173.

15. Ibid., p. 17.

16. Ibid., p. 10.

17. Ibid., p. 11.

18. This figure is an average. One should not interpret it to mean that the crime rate in each category is double the reported figure. Certainly the percentage of murders unreported would be less than double, while the percentage of aggravated assaults or robberies would more likely be at least double. The number of rapes has been estimated in some studies to be nearly four times the reported figure. See Mulvihill, Tumin, and Curtis, *Crimes of Violence, Vol. 2,* p. 19.

19. Mulvihill, Tumin, and Curtis, *Crimes of Violence, Vol. 2,* p. 26.

20. Ibid., p. 19.

Notes

21. U.S. Department of Justice, Law Enforcement Assistance Administration, "Criminal Victimization Surveys in Eight American Cities," National Criminal Justice Information and Statistics Service No. SD-NCS-C-5, November 1976, p. 1.

22. Alfred St. Louis, "Victims of Crime in Texas," *The 1976 Texas Crime Trend Survey,* (Austin, Texas: Texas Department of Public Safety, December 1976) p. 6.

23. Ibid., p. 18.

24. U.S. Department of Justice, Law Enforcement Assistance Administration, "Criminal Victimization in the United States, A Comparison of 1974 and 1975 Findings," National Criminal Justice Information and Statistics Service, No. SD-NCP-N-5, February 1977, p. 18.

25. Ibid., p. 18.

26. Ibid., p. 19.

27. "Criminal Victimization Surveys in Eight American Cities," p. 1.

CHAPTER 3

1. Judy Klemesrud, *New York Times,* 12 Nov. 1976, p. B6.

2. Robert Reiff, "Final Report of the Crime Victims Consultation Project." Submitted to the Criminal Justice Coordinating Council of New York City, September 1975.

3. Gerald Astor, "Crime Doesn't Pay Its Victims Very Well Either," *New York Times,* 30 May 1976, p. E9.

4. New York State Crime Victims Compensation Board (CVCB), *1976–1977* A Review of Tenth Year of Operation, p. 4.

5. Reiff, "Final Report," p. 40.

6. Ibid., p. 69.

7. William Claiborne, "Massive Government Help Needed for Crime Victims," *The Washington Post,* 8 Jan. 1976, p. A11.

CHAPTER 4

1. United States Department of Justice, Federal Bureau of Investigation, *Crime in the United States—1976,* Uniform Crime Reports (UCR), (Washington, D. C.: U. S. Government Printing Office, 1977), pp. 13–21.

2. Norval Morris and Gordon Hawkins, *The Honest Politician's Guide to Crime Control* (Chicago: University of Chicago Press, 1970), p. 91.

3. Del Martin, *Battered Wives* (San Francisco: Glide Publications, 1976), p. 93.

4. Martin, *Battered Wives,* p. 94.

5. *Austin American Statesman,* "Wife Beating Called More Frequent Than Rape," 21 Feb. 1978, p. A1.

6. Martin, *Battered Wives,* pp. 90–91.

7. Martin, *Battered Wives,* p. 91.

8. Martin, *Battered Wives,* p. 105.

Notes

9. Morris and Hawkins, *The Honest Politician's Guide,* p. 87.

10. Judy Klemesrud, *New York Times,* 13 Nov. 1976, p. 11.

11. Judy Klemesrud, *New York Times,* 12 Nov. 1976, p. B6.

12. Joe Frolik, "Suspended Deputy wants To File Charges," *Austin American Statesman,* 22 Feb. 1978, p. B2.

13. William Claiborne, "Threat Seen in Police Use of Hypnosis" *The Washington Post,* 8 May 1977, p. A2.

14. Leslie Maitland, "10 Rape Victims Identify Youth They All Feared to See Again," *New York Times,* 24 May 1977, p. 1.

15. Klemesrud, *New York Times,* 13 Nov. 1976, p. 11.

16. Arthur Rosett and Donald R. Cressey, *Justice by Consent* (Philadelphia: J.B. Lippincott, 1976) p. 22.

17. Rosett and Cressey, *Justice by Consent,* p. 55.

18. Pranay Gupte, "Politicians and Judges Criticized at Rally Decrying Rise in Crime," *New York Times,* 23 Feb. 1977, p. B3.

19. C. Wright Mills, *Power, Politics, and People* (New York: Oxford University Press, 1970), p. 298.

20. Everett Cherrington Hughes, *Men and Their Work* (Glencoe, Ill.: Free Press, 1958), p. 70.

21. Lesley Oelsner, "Coleman Asserts Bar Fails Public," *New York Times,* 8 Aug. 1976, p. 25.

22. New York State Crime Victims Compensation Board, pp. 10–11.

CHAPTER 5

1. Stephen Schafer, *Compensation and Restitution to Victims of Crime,* (Montclair, N.J.: Patterson Smith, 1970) pp. 128–129.

2. Letter to the Editor, *Austin American Statesman,* 15 Sep. 1977, p. A14.

3. Arthur J. Goldberg in the preface to "Symposium: Governmental Compensation for Victims of Violence, "*Southern California Law Review* 43, (1970): 1, 1–3. Quoted in Schafer, *Compensation and Restitution to Victims of Crime,* p. 151.

CHAPTER 6

1. Margery Fry, *Arms of the Law* (London: Gollancz Ltd., 1951) p. 22.

2. Fry, *Arms of the Law,* p. 24.

3. Homer, *The Iliad,* trans. W. H. D. Rouse (New York: New American Library, 1950), p. 114.

4. Ronald L. Goldfarb and Lina R. Singer, *After Conviction* (New York: Simon and Schuster, 1973), pp. 131–132.

5. Fry, *Arms of the Law,* p. 32.

6. William Tallack, *Reparations to the Injured and the Rights of the Victims to Compensation* (London: 1900), pp. 10–11. Quoted in Stephen Schafer, *Compensation and Restitution to Victims of Crime* (Montclair, N.J.: Patterson Smith, 1970), p. 8.

Notes

7. Fry, *Arms of the Law,* p. 26.

8. Fry, *Arms of the Law,* p. 26.

9. Schafer, *Compensation and Restitution,* p. 121.

10. Schafer, *Compensation and Restitution,* p. 104–105.

11. LeRoy L. Lamborn, "The Propriety of Governmental Compensation of Victims of Crime" *George Washington Law Review 41* (March 1973): 446–470.

12. Fry, *Arms of the Law,* p. 124.

13. The President's Commission on Law Enforcement and the Administration of Justice, Task Force Report: Crime and Its Impact—An Assessment" (Washington, D.C.: U.S. Government Printing Office, 1967).

14. Herbert Edelhertz and Gilbert Geis, *Public Compensation to Victims of Crime* (New York: Praeger Publishers, 1974), p. 84.

15. William L. Prosser, *Handbook of the Law of Torts,* 3rd ed. (St. Paul, Minn.: West Publishing Co., 1964), p. 331.

16. Glenn B. Martin, "Victim Compensation in Several States," Master's thesis, Lyndon B. Johnson School of Public Affairs, University of Texas at Austin, 1978, p. 78.

17. Daniel Evans, *When Crime Strikes,* State Printing Plant, Olympia, Wash., 1974. Cited in Glenn B. Martin, "Victim Compensation in Several States: A Comparative Analysis," Master's thesis, Lyndon B. Johnson School of Public Affairs, University of Texas at Austin, 1978, p. 31.

18. Violent Crimes Compensation Act, Alaska Statutes Supplement, Chapter 203, Section 18.18.010. Cited in Martin, "Victim Compensation," p. 32.

19. Kentucky Revised Statutes, Chapter 346, Section .010. Cited in Martin, Victims *Compensation,* p. 33.

20. New York State Crime Victims Compensation Board, *1976–1977 A Review of Tenth Year Operations,* p. 3.

21. Ibid., p. 4.

22. Kentucky Revised Statutes, Chapter 346, Section .010.

23. Martin, *Victim Compensation,* p. 49.

24. New York State Crime Victims Compensation Board, p. 21.

25. Ibid.

26. Martin, *Victim Compensation,* p. 53.

27. Ibid., p. 54.

28. New York State Crime Victims Compensation Board, p. 8.

29. Martin, *Victims Compensation,* p. 67.

30. Ibid., p. 75.

31. Ibid.

32. Ibid., p. 56.

CHAPTER 7

1. Jane Knitzer of the Children's Defense Fund was the first to point out the inherent political nature of advocacy in her critique of the "Report of the Joint Commission on Mental Health of Children" in her article: Jane Knitzer, "Advocacy and the Children's Crisis," *American Journal of Orthopsychiatry* 41 (5), Oct. 1971, p. 805. I have adapted some of her ideas about advocacy for children that also apply to victims of violent crime.

Notes

2. Ibid., p. 806.

3. Kenneth Carlson, Lewis Morris, Robert Spangenberg, Debra Whitcomb, "Citizens Court Watching: the Consumer Perspective." Prepared for the National Institute of Law Enforcement and Criminal Justice, Law Enforcement Assistance Administration, U.S. Department of Justice by Abt Association Inc., Oct. 1977, p. 2.

4. Ibid.

5. Fred Ferretti, "Crimes Against Elderly Bring Aged and Youths Into Court as Monitors," *New York Times,* 28 July 1977, p. B2.

6. Knitzer, "Advocacy and the Children's Crisis," p. 804.

7. Robert Reiff and Frank Riessman, *The Indigenous Non-Professional,* Community Mental Health Journal Monograph Series no. 1 (New York: Behavioral Publications, 1965), p. 14.

8. Reiff and Riessman, *The Indigenous Non-Professional,* p. 17.

9. New York Crime Victims Compensation Board.

10. Knitzer, "Advocacy and the Children's Crisis," p. 802.

CHAPTER 8

1. Donald J. Mulvihill, Melvin M. Tumin, Lynn A. Curtis *Crimes of Violence,* Vol. 2, Staff Report to the National Commission on the Causes and Prevention of Violence (Washington, D.C.: U.S. Government Printing Office, December 1969), p. 27.

2. Thorsten Sellin and Marvin Wolfgang, *The Measurement of Delinquency* (New York: John Wiley, 1964). Cited in Mulvihill, Tumin, and Curtis, *Crimes of Violence,* p. 27.

3. Ibid.

4. Ibid., p. 29.

5. Donald G. McNeil, Jr., "Carter Approves Emergency Help for Love Canal," *New York Times,* 8 Aug. 1978, p. A1.

INDEX

Index

bureaucratic indifference *(continued)*
services and, 65; victimization and, 21, 46–47, 57, 76, 107–9, 145
burglary, 18, 19, 37
Burns, Gov. John, 143
"Busse" (compensation), 136

California: victim compensation in, 156
canvassing, 43
Carey, Gov. Hugh, 8, 198
Carter, President Jimmy, 8, 197–99, 200
Center for Studies in Criminal Justice, 77, 80
Center for Study of Social Intervention, 35
centralized direct service model, 71
Chicago, 77, 199
child abuse, 151, 164
Christie, Agatha, 3
cities: as disaster areas, 193–94, 199; attitude toward police in, 92–93; high crime areas of, 4, 5, 9, 33, 36–37, 41, 46; police attitude in, 85–86, 87–88
citizen's arrest, 82–83, 122
civil suits, 84, 101, 137, 139, 198
Clairborne, William, 74
Code of Hammurabi, 134
Coleman, William T., 102
Collins, Arthur, 143
"Columbo," 6
community: effect of crime on, 201; guilt in, 132; loss due to crime, 30, 194–96; responsiveness of, 10; support systems in, 10, 194; victim outreach in, 43, 44
Community Service Corporation, 59
compensation: as welfare, 137, 141–42, 150; "Bot," Saxon payment of, 134; "Busse," 136; compared with Workman's Compensation, 139–40, 142; eligibility for, 140, 145–46; federal support of, 139; historical review of, 134–35; rationales for, 15, 140–42; state laws for, 15, 62, 139
condition of life, *see* stoicism

Congress, 8, 14, 15, 17
Consolidated Edison, 8
constitutional rights, 97, 103, 117–18
convictions: assault, 26–27, 28; lesser charge, 25, 26, 27, 28; murder, 26, 28; percentage of violent crime resulting in, 29; rape, 27, 28; robbery, 27–28
Co-op City News, 43
Co-op City Times, 43
counseling, 59
counselors: paraprofessionals as, 38, 39; victim contact by, 40, 43, 44, 60, 71; *see also* victim-advocate
Court Appearance Control Project, 59, 70
court monitoring, 178, 180–81
court reform: proposals for, 115–22
crime: as social problem, 86–87, 113; failure to report, 20–21, 128; punishment as deterrent to, 24–25, 29, 113; victimless, 18, 87
crime index: crime categories in, 18, 23, 25, 28, 29, 30; on seriousness of crime, 19, 29–30, 195
"crime in the house," 51
"crime in the streets," 33, 51, 199
crime prevention programs, 44
crime rate: failure to reveal extent of, 17–18, 21, 196; social problems and, 194; true, 7, 20, 29, 34
crime reporting: by FBI, 18–35; inaccuracy of, 19, 196
crime statistics: 17–35
crime victim, *see* victim
crime victim compensation, 139–46; administrative structure of, 165–67; application for, 155, 160–64; cost of program for, 167–74; discrepancies in state laws for, 146–62; effectiveness of, 144–46; familial exclusion in, 151–53; for survivors, 156–59 (chart); limitations, 156–59 (chart); public awareness of, 153–55; rationale of state laws for, 146–47; suggestions for effectiveness of, 163–65, 174–75; welfare concept of, 145–50, 162
Crime Victims Advocacy Center: budget and operation of 73–74; goals of, 72–73

Index

Index

Index

Index

Metropolitan Hospital, 45
Michigan: victim compensation in, 149, 151, 155, 157, 165, 166, 170, 172
Middle Ages, 132, 134–35
Mills, C. Wright, 100
Minnesota: victim compensation in, 157
Miranda-type notice, 154–55
misdemeanor, 20, 196–97
Morris, Norval, 77, 86
Morrison, Edward A., 63
Mosholu Library, 45
"most serious" crime, 19, 20, 32
Mount Eden Center, 89
mugging, 51, 88
multiple crimes: UCR reporting of, 19–20; LEAA reporting of, 32
multi-problem population, 46, 56–57; needs of, 70–71
murder, 30, 31, 48; arrests for, 23; convictons for, 26; crime rate for, 7; family and, 22, 38; prosecutions, 26; UCR definition of, 18; see also homicide

Nader, Ralph, 102–3
National Commission on Causes and Prevention of Violence, 30, 195
National Crime Survey Program, 31
National Opinion Research Center (NORC), 31
natural disaster: aid to victims of, 9–10; compared with violent crime, 7; definition of, 199; human response to, 10–11; social attitudes toward, 12, 15–16
needs of victims: data on 36–57; definition by welfare worker of, 64; proposed changes to meet, 65–74; retrospective view of, 64; reactive view of, 64; services available for, 58–63
needs test, 62, 147, 148, 149
neighborhood safety: programs for, 44
New Jersey, 15; victim compensation in, 157
newspaper: publicity in, 42, 43
New York, 199; victim compensation in, 146, 148, 150, 151, 155, 158, 160, 164, 165, 170, 172, 173, 174
New York City, 36, 38, 49, 70, 72; blackout in, 8, 197
New York State Crime Victims Compensation Board, 109–10, 190; application to, 161; eligibility for, 148; responsiveness of, 60–63
New York State Legislative Commission on Expenditure Review, 62
New York State Senate, 62
New York Times, 43
Niagara Falls, N.Y., 198
Nickerson, Rev. Daniel, 5
Nigeria, 132–33
nonnegligent manslaughter, 18
North Dakota: victim compensation in, 158

Oelsner, Lesley, 102–3
offender: advantages of postponement for, 96–97, 119–20; court monitoring projects for, 179; criminal justice systems as an encouragement to, 105–6; determination of, 12; economic status of, 137–38; familial relationship of, 21, 50; focus of media on, 6; historical view of, 131–36; intimidation of victim by, 5; known to police, 77; plea-bargaining as denial of rights of, 97; police discretion and the, 20, 122; public attitude as encouragement of, 93; probability of conviction of, 25; reducing blame on, 13–14; restitution as benefit to, 138; restitution as a responsibility of, 115–17, 196–97; restitution by, 137–38; 167–69; treatment of ghetto residents as potential, 81, 87; treatment of victim compared with, 75–76, 78–79 (chart)
offenses, 22, 28; murder, 23; prosecuted, 23–24; lesser, 25; rape, 27; aggravated assault, 26–27; robbery, 27; studies based on the number of, 32
Ohio: victim compensation in, 158
ombudsman (advocate), 118

Index

outreach services to contact victims, 42–44, 69

Pang, Wilfred S., 171
pamphlets and posters for CVSC, 43
paraprofessionals, 38, 66
Parkchester News, 43
Pennsylvania: victim compensation in, 158
personal crime, 20–21, 83–85
physical harm, 3–4, 29, 38, 53, 56, *see also* injury
physical health: needs of victim, 34, 52, 54, 56
physical injury: effects of, 5
Planned Parenthood, 45
plea-bargaining, 96–99, 104, 117
police: accountability of, 67, 123; attitude toward offender, 20, 77, 88, 93, 122; attitude toward victims, 37, 67–68, 87–88, 92–94, 123; consciousness-raising of, 93–95, 126; court appearances of, 97, 121; crime statistics and, 19, 51; discretionary power of, 76–77, 80–83, 122–23; domestic quarrels and, 80; effect of high crime rate upon, 87–88; homicide arrests and the, 25–26; issue of victim's rights and, 122; media view of, 6; morale of, 89–90; procedure for dealing with needs of victims, 67–68; protection of public, 21, 85, 194; public attitude toward, 85–86, 92–93; reporting of crime, 19, 20; responsibility toward elderly, 128; role in plea-bargaining, 98; training, 89–90; training in hypnosis, 90–92; treatment of public nuisance, 88
Police Senior Citizens Robbery Unit, 4, 11, 93–94, 126
Police Training Academy, Michigan, 80–81
politicians: and public opinion, 15, 177
poor neighborhoods: relationship to high crime rate, 5, 49, 51; South Bronx as, 46; victimization rates in, 33–34; viewed as disaster areas, 193–94

poor people, 194; and stoicism, 41, 65; and the legal profession, 101–4; as multi-problem families, 46; bureaucratic treatment of, 46–47; frequency of crime among, 4; life style of, 5, 46–47; study of victims among, 37; victimization among, 37; victimization rate of, 33–34
post-crime victimization, 37, 75–100; and loss of property, 126; by bureaucracy, 107–8; caused by discrepencies in compensation, 147; reforms to prevent, 113–30; victim advocacy to prevent, 176–77, 181, 186–87
postponements: 80, 96–97; advance notice of, 121; reform in practice of, 67, 119–20
President's Commission on Law Enforcement and Administration of Justice, 141
private vengeance, 131, 133, 135–36
probability of violent crime, 6–7
probable cause, 77, 80
property crimes, 18, 19, 30, 33, 34, 37, 46
prosecutions, 23–24, 28; for aggravated assault, 26–27; for murder, 25–26; for rape, 27; for robbery, 27–28; percentage resulting in convictions, 25
prostitution, 18, 87
protection, *see* safety
protection order, 123–25; *see also* restraining order
provocation, 160; concept of, 12–13, 88
psychiatrists, 46, 92
psychologists, 46, 92
public assistance, *see* welfare
publicity, 42–44, 62, 63, 153
public opinion, 15, 176, 200
public vengeance, 131–32, 134, 135–36
punishment: as deterrent to crime, 24, 29; historical concept of state and, 134–35; restitution and, 136–38

Index

racial background of victim, 47–48, 49, 50–51; in arrests, 22; of convictions, 39
racial balance, 48
racial hostility, 49
radio: as outreach to victims, 42, 43, 47
rape, 5, 38, 48, 164; conviction rate for, 25; crime rate for, 7, 28, 77; eligibility for compensation for, 150, 151; emotional recall of, 91–92; index of seriousness of, 195; prevention and education service, 11, 44–45, 67; provocation and, 13–14; true crime rate for, 21, 31; UCR definition of, 18
rape victim advocate, 45
reactive view, 64
reasonable belief, 77, 80
referrals: to Crime Victims Compensation Board, 38–39, 45–46, 48, 60–63; to service agencies, 58–60; victims' attitudes toward, 65–66
rehabilitation: of offender, 182; of neighborhoods, 193, 199–200, 201
Reiser, Martin, 90
rent control, 49
reparation, *see* restitution
reprisal, *see* retaliation
restitution, 70, 136–38; as concept "being made whole," 75–76, 107, 112–14, 116, 134, 146, 147, 149; as right of victim, 135–36; historical concepts, 133–36; offender and, 137–38; to victim, 115–17, 193; to state, 134
restraining order, 83–84, *see also* protection order
retaliation, 5, 21, 65, 70
retrospective view, 31–32, 35, 38, 64
revenge: historical concept of, 131–32, 133
revictimization: by offender, 5, 60, 128; by bureaucracy, 65, 108, 124; information about, 35; by police, 93–94
rights of victim: for aid, 16, 177; for information, 125; for justice, 111–12, 200, 201
rituals: human behavior and, 131–32

robbery: crime rate for, 7, 21, 27–28, 31, 51, 77; in Code of Hammurabi, 134; UCR definition of, 18
Rockefeller, Gov. Nelson, 143
Rodino, Congressman Peter W., Jr., 15, 139, 153

safety: isolation as, 41, 68; lack of, 5, 21, 123; legal protection and, 55, 60, 70, 128; relocation and, 56; right to, 84–85
San Francisco, 82
Schafer, Stephan, 136
Science and Technology Task Force, 195
Seattle, 83
Sellin, Thorsten, 195
sexual assault, *see* rape
shock, 4, 5, 42
Siegel, Bill, 88
Silverman, Irvin, 88
Simon, Abe, 127
Simonson, Archie, 13
Small Business Administration, 8, 197
Smith, Chesterfield, 103
social attitudes: and natural disaster, 10–11; toward police, 85–86; toward victim aid, 11–12, 14
socialism, 14
social justice: historical view of, 129, 131–138; responsibility for, 16, 106, 169, 193, 200; victim's need for, 15; victim's right to, 75–76, 107, 112–114, 129
social security, 53, 58
social tragedy, 194; crime as, 162
social welfare agencies: failure to classify victims in, 68; lack of utilization by victims, 65–66, 143; referrals to, 58–60; responsiveness of 58, 60; victim advocacy and, 38, 176, 177–78; *see also* health services agencies
social worker, 46
South Bronx, 46, 49, 94
Spanish, 40, 42, 43, 61, 63, 153
special status classification of victims, 68–69, 71
Specific Data Projects, 179

Index

State: as wronged, 134
State Crime Victim Compensation Boards, 14
State Crime Victim Compensation Laws, 14, 156–59 (chart); administration of, 165–74; application for, 155, 160–63; eligibility for, 147–50; familial exclusion, 151–53; federal aid for, 15; minimum loss, 150–51; public awareness of, 153–55; rationale, 146–47; recommendations for, 163–65, 174–75
statistics: computerized accounting of, 200; on crime, 17–35; on seriousness of crime, 194–96
statutory rape, 18
Stein, Lily, 93–94
Stern, Michael, 180
stoicism, 41, 65, 145
Sudiker, Barry, 98–99
suicide, 4, 18
survey of victim needs, 31–35, 38, 64
suspicion, 5, 41, 65

taboo, 132
telephone: contact with victim by, 40–41, 42, 44
television and other media: publicity on service to victims, 43, 44, 47; focus on offender, 6; view of poverty, 5
Tennessee: victim compensation in, 159
terror, 3, 21, 50, 65, 123
Texas: law enforcement training in, 89–90
theft, 18, 19, 33, 129
translation assistance, 58, 59, 61, 63
trials: convictions as a result of, 25–28; court appearance for, 59, 70, 97, 121; court-monitoring of, 96, 178, 180; court reform and, 115–22; day care for mothers during, 121; escort and protection services related to, 59, 70, 84, 94, 128; postponement of, 67, 80, 96–97, 119–20, 121; legal aid and, 60
Tried Stone Baptist Church, 5

Truninger, Elizabeth, 82
Twersky, Ziporah, 74

unemployment: aid as welfare, 14; services for, 197
Uniform Crime Report (UCR), 17–19, 22–29, 30–32, 140–41, 195; true crime rate and, 21–22
United States: crime rate in, 6–9, 17–18
University of Chicago, 31
urban crime, *see* cities
utilization of services, 41, 42, 65, 145

vandalism, 108, 194, 199
vendetta, 133
vengeance, historical view of, 131–32
Victim: advocacy to aid, 72, 176–92; attitudes of, 41–42, 47, 48, 65, 144; brutal treatment of, 5, 29–30, 49; bureaucratic attitude toward, 46–47, 57; compensation for, 14, 60–63, 139–46, 147–53, 164; court appearance of, 39, 40, 55, 59, 60, 96–97, 99, 119–21; court postponements and, 96–97; crime rate and, 17–18, 22, 29; emotional needs of, 64; emotional trauma of, 3–4; failure to report crime, 19, 21; familial exclusion in compensation for, 63, 151–53; family of, 22; fear and, *see* fear; financial aid for, 62–63, 67; frustration of, 20; health service agencies and, 4, 107–9; historical view of, 131–36; housing needs of, 9, 196; intimidation of, 5, 60, 125; invisibility of, 5, 6, 37, 39, 65; isolation of, 5–6, 21, 123; lawyers and, 101, 106; legal aid for, 67; legal services for, 117–19; life style of, 21, 47, 123; loss to, 30, 34; media view of, 6; medical care for, 67; middle class as, 33, 48, 81, 141–42, 149; Miranda-type notice for, 154–55; needs of, 36–57, 64; needs test for, 62, 147, 148, 149; offender related to,

217

Index

Index

women: battered, 50, 80–81, 83–84, 123; court appearances and, 99; rape instruction and, 11

Women's Litigation Unit of San Fran-

cisco Neighborhood Legal Assistance Foundation, 82

Workman's Compensation, 55, 61, 139–40, 142